# The AI Wealth Creation Bible

## Step-by-Step Guide to
## AI-Driven Financial Success

*Malik Harris*

# Download Your 3 Bonus Chapters On **Vital 2025 Information** Here!

# Table of Contents

# Chapter 1: Introduction to Artificial Intelligence

Artificial intelligence (AI) is one of the most fascinating and promising technologies of our time. But what does "artificial intelligence" really mean? How did this technology come about, and what are the basic concepts that make it so powerful? In this chapter, we will explore the definition of AI, its fundamental concepts, and take a brief journey through its history and evolution.

## 1.1 Definition of Artificial Intelligence

When we talk about artificial intelligence, we refer to the ability of machines to perform tasks that, if done by humans, would require the application of human intelligence. These tasks include voice recognition, problem-solving, learning, and planning. Essentially, AI enables computers and devices to "think" and "learn" in a manner similar to humans. Imagine having a virtual assistant that not only follows your voice commands but also learns from your habits and helps you organize your daily life better. This is an example of AI. It may seem magical, it may seem hard to believe, but it is, in fact, the result of sophisticated algorithms and the analysis of vast amounts of data.

The definition of AI can vary depending on the context. In simple terms, AI is a technology that allows machines to learn from experience, adapt to new inputs, and perform human-like tasks. It is based on algorithms and mathematical models that enable computers to carry out activities requiring human intelligence, such as recognizing images, understanding natural language, and making decisions.

## 1.2 Basic Concepts of AI

To understand how AI works, you don't need to be a tech expert. However, having a basic knowledge of some key concepts can be very helpful.

### Machine Learning

Machine learning is the heart of AI. Instead of being programmed to perform specific tasks, computers use algorithms to "learn" from data. For example, a music streaming app can suggest new songs based on your previous listening choices. This happens because the algorithm has analyzed your music preferences and learned to predict what you might like. In practice, machine learning can be compared to human learning. Just as we learn from our mistakes and experiences, a machine learning system uses past data to improve its future predictions. This continuous learning process allows AI to become increasingly accurate and useful over time.

### Neural Networks

Neural networks are mathematical models inspired by the human brain. These models help machines recognize patterns and make predictions. If you have ever used facial recognition on your smartphone, you have experienced a neural network in action. Your phone analyzes the features of your face and compares them to a database to confirm your identity. Neural networks consist of layers of artificial neurons that work together to process information. Each layer of the neural network processes data differently, allowing the network to recognize increasingly complex features. For example, the first layers of a neural network analyzing images may identify simple edges and shapes, while subsequent layers can recognize more complex objects like faces or cars.

### Natural Language Processing (NLP)

NLP enables computers to understand and respond to human language. This is what makes it possible to converse with virtual assistants like Siri or Alexa. Thanks to NLP, these assistants can understand your requests and respond appropriately. NLP involves various techniques that allow computers to analyze, understand, and generate human language. For instance, when you ask Siri to set an alarm, NLP is used to analyze your request, understand the meaning, and respond with the appropriate action. This process includes tokenization (breaking the text into words), syntactic analysis (understanding the sentence structure), and semantic analysis (understanding the meaning of the words).

### Computer Vision

Computer vision allows computers to interpret and understand images and videos. This tool is used in many applications, such as self-driving cars, which must "see" and interpret the surrounding environment to move safely. Computer vision uses algorithms to analyze images and videos, identify objects, detect movements, and understand complex scenes. For example, a computer vision system can be used in a supermarket to monitor shelves and alert when a product is about to run out. Similarly, security cameras with computer vision can detect suspicious behavior and alert operators.

## 1.3 History and Evolution of AI

AI is not a novelty of the twenty-first century, even though it might seem so; it has a rich and fascinating history. Let's take a brief look at the key milestones of this tool that will increasingly revolutionize our lives.

## 1950s: The Dawn of AI

The term "artificial intelligence" was coined in 1956 by John McCarthy, one of the pioneers in the field. During a conference at Dartmouth, McCarthy and other scientists discussed the possibility of creating machines capable of thinking like humans. During these years, the first AI programs were developed, capable of solving mathematical problems and playing chess. At this time, AI was seen as an academic curiosity. Scientists were fascinated by the idea of creating machines that could simulate human intelligence, but the technological capabilities of the era were limited. However, these early experiments laid the foundation for the future development of AI.

## 1980s: AI in Action

In the 1980s, AI began to find practical applications. Expert systems were developed, designed to emulate the decision-making abilities of human experts in specific fields like medicine and engineering. These systems could analyze complex data and provide recommendations based on predefined rules. Expert systems represented a significant step forward because they demonstrated that AI could be used to solve real-world problems. For example, a medical expert system could analyze a patient's symptoms and suggest diagnoses and treatments. This type of AI was still limited by the rules and data on which it was trained, but it paved the way for further developments.

## 2000s: The Advent of Machine Learning

With the increase in computing power and the availability of large amounts of data, machine learning became the core of AI.

Machine learning algorithms allowed computers to improve their performance by analyzing large datasets. This led to innovations such as intelligent search engines and recommendation systems. Machine learning made AI more flexible and powerful, as it enabled systems to learn from data without needing to be explicitly programmed for each task. This approach led to numerous practical applications, from spam filters in email to personalized recommendations on e-commerce websites.

## Today: The Era of Advanced AI

Today, AI is present in many aspects of our daily lives. From navigation apps that optimize routes based on real-time traffic to home security systems that recognize faces and suspicious behaviors, AI continues to evolve. Research continues to push the boundaries towards new frontiers, such as the creation of general artificial intelligences that can emulate all human cognitive abilities. Advanced AI is made possible by the combination of technologies such as machine learning, deep neural networks, and natural language processing. These technologies work together to create systems that can tackle complex tasks autonomously and efficiently.

## The Future of AI

Looking ahead, the potential of AI is immense. It is expected that AI could revolutionize sectors such as healthcare, education, transportation, and many others. With the development of increasingly sophisticated technologies, AI could lead to innovations that we cannot even imagine today. For example, in the field of healthcare, AI could be used to develop personalized treatments based on a patient's genetic profile. In the transportation sector, self-driving cars could become the norm, reducing traffic and improving road safety. The possibilities are endless, and AI will continue to transform our world in surprising ways. Understanding the basic concepts and history of AI is essential for anyone looking to leverage its potential to create new income opportunities. In the upcoming chapters, we will explore how these technologies can be used to generate passive income and transform your professional life.

# Chapter 2: Market Overview and Opportunities

Artificial intelligence (AI) offers numerous opportunities to generate passive income. However, to make the most of these opportunities, it's essential to understand the digital market in which we operate. In this chapter, we will explore the digital market and its dynamics, focusing on how AI can be used to identify and leverage these opportunities.

## 2.1 Digital Market Analysis

The digital market is a vast and ever-evolving ecosystem that includes a variety of sectors, from e-commerce to social media, online advertising to streaming services. Understanding the trends and dynamics of this market is crucial for anyone looking to create passive income using AI.

### Overview of the Digital Market

In recent years, the digital market has seen exponential growth. This growth has been fueled by increased Internet access, the proliferation of mobile devices, and the adoption of new technologies. The digital market offers many opportunities to create and sell products and services online. Here are some key sectors:

1. **E-commerce:** E-commerce is one of the most dynamic sectors of the digital market. Platforms like Amazon, eBay, and Shopify have made it easier than ever for entrepreneurs to sell products globally. AI can be used to optimize e-commerce operations, such as inventory

management, product recommendation personalization, and customer service automation.

2. **Social-Media:** Social-media has become an integral part of our daily lives. Platforms like Facebook, Instagram, TikTok, and Twitter offer unique opportunities for content creation and monetization. AI can help create more engaging content, analyze trends, and improve marketing strategies.

3. **Online Advertising:** Online advertising is a growing market. Advertisers can reach a vast audience using platforms like Google Ads and Facebook Ads. AI can improve the effectiveness of advertising campaigns through precise user targeting, bid optimization, and performance analysis.

4. **Streaming Services:** Streaming services like Netflix, YouTube, and Spotify have revolutionized how we consume content. AI plays a crucial role in these platforms, helping to recommend content, personalize user experiences, and manage copyright issues.

## Current and Future Trends

The digital market is constantly evolving, driven by technological innovation and changes in consumer preferences. For those looking to create passive income by leveraging artificial intelligence, it is crucial to stay updated on current and future trends. In this subsection, we will explore some of the most relevant trends shaping the digital market and how these can offer new opportunities for profit.

## Current Trends

## 1. Growth of Mobile Commerce (m-commerce)

Mobile commerce, or m-commerce, refers to the buying and selling of goods and services through mobile devices such as smartphones and tablets. With the increasing use of mobile devices, m-commerce has become a significant part of the global e-commerce market.

- Advantages:

The convenience of shopping anytime and anywhere, immediate access to deals, and the ease of use of mobile apps.

- Opportunities:

Businesses can develop user-friendly mobile apps, optimize websites for mobile devices, and use push notifications for personalized promotions.

## 2. Automation and Artificial Intelligence

Automation, supported by AI, is transforming many aspects of the digital market. From marketing automation to inventory management, AI is making business operations more efficient and cost-effective.

- Advantages:

Reduced operational costs, increased efficiency, and improved accuracy.

- Opportunities:

Use chatbots for customer service, recommendation algorithms to personalize offers, and analytics tools to make data-driven decisions.

3. **Personalization of User Experience**

Consumers expect increasingly personalized experiences. Companies that can offer tailored content and offers based on individual customer preferences see increased loyalty and sales.

- Advantages:

Higher customer engagement, increased satisfaction, and repeat sales.

- Opportunities:

Implement recommendation systems, personalize email marketing campaigns, and use predictive analytics to anticipate customer needs.

4. **Growth of the Creator Economy**

The creator economy refers to the economy generated by individuals who create digital content and monetize it through platforms like YouTube, TikTok, Patreon, and others. These content creators are building lucrative careers by leveraging their creativity and direct access to their followers.

- Advantages:

 Direct access to the audience, ability to earn through various income streams such as ads, sponsorships, and product sales.

- Opportunities:

Create high-quality content, build a loyal follower base, and monetize through multiple platforms.

5. **Influencer Marketing**

Influencer marketing has become an essential marketing strategy for many companies. Collaborating with influencers who have a loyal following can significantly boost brand visibility and sales.

- Advantages:

Access to a targeted audience, increased brand credibility, and higher sales.

- Opportunities:
  Identify and collaborate with relevant influencers, create authentic influencer marketing campaigns, and measure the impact of collaborations.

## Future Trends

1. **Expansion of Generative Artificial Intelligence**

Generative AI, which includes the automatic creation of content such as text, images, and music, is set to become even more sophisticated. Tools like DALL-E and GPT-3 are already demonstrating the potential of this technology.

- Impact:

Faster and cheaper content creation, new forms of creative expression, and automation of creative tasks.

- Opportunities:

Develop generative AI-based tools and services for sectors such as marketing, publishing, and entertainment.

## 2. **Widespread Adoption of Augmented Reality and Virtual Reality (AR/VR)**

Augmented Reality (AR) and Virtual Reality (VR) are emerging as key technologies to enhance user experience. These technologies are finding applications in various sectors, from retail to education, tourism to video games.

- Impact:

Immersive user experiences, new ways to interact with products, and improved marketing strategies.

- Opportunities:

Create AR/VR applications for marketing, virtual shopping, and training.

## 3. **Development of IoT Ecosystems (Internet of Things)**

The Internet of Things (IoT) refers to the connection of smart devices via the Internet, allowing them to communicate and share data. This technology is set to grow, transforming homes, offices, and cities into smart environments.

- Impact:

Increased operational efficiency, improved quality of life, and new business opportunities.

- Opportunities:

Develop IoT solutions for home automation, energy management, and smart cities.

### 4. Blockchain and Smart Contracts

Blockchain is a distributed ledger technology that ensures transparency and security of transactions. Smart contracts, which automatically execute when certain conditions are met, can revolutionize many sectors, from finance to real estate.

- Impact:

More secure transactions, reduction of fraud, and automation of contractual processes.

- Opportunities:

Develop blockchain-based applications for identity management, supply chain, and payments.

### 5. Increased Ethical Awareness and Regulation

As AI and other technologies advance, there is a growing awareness of their ethical and social implications. Regulation is set to become stricter to ensure the responsible use of technology.

- Impact:

Greater transparency, data protection, and respect for privacy.

- Opportunities:

Offer consultancy on compliance and regulation, develop technological solutions that meet ethical and legal standards.

Staying updated on current and future trends in the digital market is essential for anyone looking to leverage the opportunities offered by artificial intelligence. Current trends, such as the growth of mobile commerce and personalization of the user experience, offer immediate earning opportunities. At the same time, future trends, such as the expansion of generative AI and the adoption of AR/VR, will open new frontiers and business opportunities.

# 2.2 Identifying Business Opportunities

Artificial intelligence (AI) offers a vast range of opportunities for those seeking to create new businesses or improve existing ones. However, identifying the right business opportunities requires an in-depth understanding of the digital market and its dynamics. In this subchapter, we will explore how to identify and exploit business opportunities in the context of AI, with a focus on the importance of predictive analytics.

## Market Analysis and Identifying Needs

To identify business opportunities, the first step is to understand the market and consumer needs. This process begins with market analysis, which can be divided into several phases:

1. **Market Research**

Market research is essential to understand current trends, consumer behaviors, and market gaps. Here's how you can do it:

- Data Analysis:

Use data analysis tools like Google Analytics, social media insights, and industry reports to gather information on consumer behaviors and preferences.

- Surveys and Interviews:

 Conduct surveys and interviews with your target audience to get direct feedback on their needs and desires.

- Competitor Monitoring:

Analyze your competitors' strategies to identify what works and where there are untapped opportunities.

2. **Identifying Trends**

Staying updated on emerging trends is crucial for spotting new business opportunities. Trends can be technological, market-based, or social. For example, the growing adoption of voice assistants and smart devices may indicate opportunities to develop applications or services compatible with these technologies.

3. **Market Segmentation**

Segmenting the market involves dividing the audience into smaller groups with similar characteristics. This allows you to identify market segments that may be underserved or have specific needs that have not yet been met.

## Identifying Business Opportunities: Predictive Analytics

Predictive analytics is a fundamental discipline in the field of artificial intelligence and data analysis. This advanced technology allows companies to anticipate trends, behaviors, and future outcomes based on historical data and complex mathematical models. By using machine learning algorithms and statistical techniques, predictive analytics extracts valuable insights from existing data to make accurate predictions about future events. This process is crucial for identifying new business opportunities, improving business strategies, and gaining a competitive advantage.

## How Predictive Analytics Works

### 1. Data Collection

- Data Sources:

Data collection is the first and most important step in the predictive analytics process. Data sources can include company databases, social media, IoT sensors, financial transactions, health records, and many others. The more diverse and rich the data, the better the predictions.

- Data Volume:

Big data techniques allow for the management and analysis of large volumes of data, which can reach hundreds of terabytes. The goal is to collect data that is relevant to the problem you want to solve.

### 2. Data Cleaning and Preparation

- Removing Missing or Incorrect Data:

Collected data often contains errors, duplicates, or missing values. Data cleaning involves removing or correcting these errors to ensure the predictive models are accurate.

- Normalization and Transformation:

Data must be normalized and transformed into a format suitable for analysis. This can include scaling variables, encoding categories, and aggregating time-series data.

- Feature Engineering:

This phase involves identifying and creating new variables (features) that can improve the performance of the predictive model. For example, you can create variables like seasonal trends, customer behavior indices, or complex financial metrics.

3. **Model Development**

- Algorithm Selection:

Various machine learning algorithms can be used for predictive analytics, including linear regression, decision trees, neural networks, support vector machines (SVM), and clustering algorithms. The choice of algorithm depends on the type of data and the specific problem.

- Model Training:

 The model is trained using a training dataset. During this phase, the algorithm learns from historical data by identifying patterns and relationships.

- Model Validation:

After training, the model is tested on a test dataset to evaluate its accuracy. This step is essential to avoid overfitting and ensure the model performs well on unseen data.

### 4. Model Validation and Optimization

- Cross-Validation:

Cross-validation is a technique used to evaluate the robustness of the model. It involves splitting the data into multiple segments and training/testing the model on different combinations of these segments.

- Hyperparameter Optimization:

Hyperparameters are parameters that must be set before training the model. Hyperparameter optimization involves finding the optimal values that improve the model's performance.

- Evaluation Metrics:

Model performance is evaluated using metrics such as accuracy, precision-recall, area under the ROC curve (AUC-ROC), and mean squared error (MSE).

### 5. Implementation and Monitoring

- Implementation in Business Systems:

Once validated, the predictive model is implemented in business systems. This can include integration with business intelligence (BI) platforms, marketing campaign management tools, or supply chain management software.

- Continuous Monitoring:

After implementation, it is essential to monitor the model's performance over time. The model may require periodic updates or retraining to adapt to new data and maintain prediction accuracy.

- Maintenance and Update:

Market conditions and business dynamics constantly change. Predictive models must be regularly updated and retrained to reflect these new realities.

## Applications of Predictive Analytics

Predictive analytics has applications in numerous sectors, offering significant advantages in terms of operational efficiency, strategy improvement, and profitability enhancement.

1. **Marketing**

- Campaign Personalization:

Predict customer behavior to personalize advertising campaigns and improve marketing strategy effectiveness.

- Market Segmentation:

Use demographic and behavioral data to segment the market and target specific customer groups with tailored offers.

## 2. Finance

- Risk Management:

Predict credit risks and financial fraud to protect financial institutions and improve risk management.

- Portfolio Optimization:

Use predictive models to optimize portfolio management and forecast investment performance.

## 3. Healthcare

- Early Diagnosis:

Anticipate epidemics and improve early disease diagnosis through the analysis of health data.

- Resource Management:

Predict the demand for healthcare resources and optimize hospital and clinic management.

## 4. E-commerce

- Sales Forecasting:

Predict future sales to better manage inventory and optimize logistics operations.

- Product Recommendations:

Use predictive models to suggest products to customers based on their past purchasing behavior.

5. **Manufacturing**

- Predictive Maintenance:

Optimize the supply chain and predict equipment failures to reduce downtime and improve operational efficiency.

- Production Optimization:

Use production data to optimize manufacturing processes and reduce waste.

Predictive analytics represents one of the most powerful and versatile technologies in the modern business arsenal. By integrating these advanced techniques into decision-making processes, companies can not only improve their daily operations but also anticipate future trends and identify new growth opportunities. With the right combination of data, technology, and skills, predictive analytics can transform how businesses operate, leading to greater efficiency, profitability, and innovation.

## AI-Based Business Opportunities

Once you understand the market and identify consumer needs, the next step is to explore how AI can be used to meet those needs. Here are some areas where AI offers significant opportunities:

1. **Business Process Automation**

- Inventory Management:

Use AI to predict demand and optimize inventory levels.

- Customer Support:

Implement chatbots that automatically respond to customer inquiries, improving service and reducing the need for human staff.

- Data Analysis:

Leverage machine learning algorithms to analyze large volumes of data and gain useful insights for business decisions.

## 2. Personalizing the User Experience

Personalization is a powerful tool to enhance customer engagement and loyalty. AI can help create highly personalized experiences through:

- Product Recommendations:

Use recommendation algorithms to suggest products based on customers' preferences and past behaviors.

- Targeted Marketing:

Develop personalized marketing campaigns that reach the right customers with the right message at the right time.

- Custom Content:

Create content that meets the specific needs of each user, enhancing the overall experience.

## 3. Developing Innovative Products and Services

AI offers the potential to develop entirely new products and services that were previously impossible. Examples include:

- Augmented Reality (AR) Applications:

Create AR experiences that enhance how consumers interact with products.

- AI-Based Consulting Services:

Offer specialized consulting in various sectors, such as healthcare, finance, and education, using AI tools to provide data-driven insights and recommendations.

- E-learning Platforms:

Develop online learning platforms that use AI to personalize learning paths and improve student outcomes.

4. **Monetizing Digital Content**

Creating and monetizing digital content is an area where AI can make a significant difference. Here are some ideas:

- Automated Content Creation:

Use AI tools to generate articles, blog posts, videos, and other digital content.

- Content Optimization:

Leverage AI to analyze the effectiveness of content and optimize it to improve engagement and conversions.

- Selling Premium Content:

Offer exclusive paid content, such as online courses, e-books, or video tutorials.

Identifying business opportunities in the digital market requires careful market analysis, understanding emerging trends, and strategic use of artificial intelligence. Whether you aim to automate business processes, personalize user experiences, or develop innovative new products, AI offers powerful tools to achieve your goals. In the following chapters, we will explore how to implement these strategies and make the most of AI technologies to create a successful business and generate passive income.

# Chapter 3: Tools and Technologies for AI

As it is widely discussed globally and deeply explored in this book, artificial intelligence (AI) is revolutionizing how businesses and professionals operate in the digital world. Thanks to AI-based tools and platforms, it is possible to automate complex processes, improve operational efficiency, create high-quality content, and analyze data with unprecedented accuracy. This chapter will explore a wide range of AI tools and platforms that are essential for anyone wishing to fully leverage the potential of AI.

In this chapter, we will focus on four main categories of AI tools and technologies: major AI platforms, artificial intelligence software, automation tools, and social and content platforms. Each section will provide a detailed overview of the features, benefits, and usage of each tool, offering a practical guide to integrating these technologies into your daily activities.

It is important to note that most of the tools and platforms described in this chapter will be functional for income-generating activities through the use of artificial intelligence, as described in the following Chapter 4. We will learn how to use these advanced technologies to create passive income streams, optimize content creation, enhance marketing and sales campaigns, and much more. Whether you are an emerging entrepreneur or an experienced professional, these tools will provide you with the technological foundations necessary to succeed in the AI era.

## 3.1 Major AI Platforms

# Tenweb.io

Tenweb.io is a platform that uses artificial intelligence to simplify and accelerate the website creation process. It offers a wide range of customizable templates and automation tools for site maintenance, making it easier for users to focus on content and the growth of their online business. Tenweb.io is ideal for entrepreneurs and small businesses looking for a professional online presence without the need for advanced technical skills.

Key Features:

- Automatic website generation
- Intuitive design tools
- Automatic SEO optimization
- Integration with various plugins and third-party services

How to Use:

1. Sign up on Tenweb.io and choose a website template.
2. Customize the design using visual editing tools.
3. Add content and optimize the site for search engines.
4. Publish the site and use the automatic maintenance tools to keep it updated.

# MidJourney

MidJourney is an AI platform specialized in creating digital art. Using advanced machine learning algorithms, MidJourney allows users to generate unique, high-quality images, perfect for artistic projects, digital graphics, and even NFTs (Non-Fungible Tokens).

Key Features:

- Image generation from textual descriptions
- Wide range of available artistic styles
- Integration with NFT sales platforms
- Image editing and customization tools

How to Use:

1. Access MidJourney and create an account.
2. Provide a textual description of the image you want to create.
3. Use the customization tools to refine the generated image.
4. Export the image for use in your projects or for sale as an NFT.

# DALL-E

DALL-E, developed by OpenAI, is one of the most advanced AI-based image generators. Capable of creating realistic and artistic images from textual descriptions, DALL-E is a powerful tool for artists, designers, and marketers looking to create unique visual content.

Key Features:

- Creation of images from detailed textual descriptions

- Support for a wide range of artistic styles

- High resolution and quality of generated images

- Easy integration with other design tools

How to Use:

1. Sign up with OpenAI and access DALL-E.

2. Enter a detailed textual description of the image you want to create.

3. Refine the image using the available customization options.

4. Export the image for use in your creative or marketing projects.

## Leonardo AI

Leonardo AI is a versatile platform that combines artificial intelligence and machine learning to offer advanced solutions in various sectors, including digital marketing, data analysis, and business process automation.

Key Features:

- Advanced data analysis tools

- Business process automation

- Customizable machine learning algorithms

- Integration with marketing and CRM platforms

How to Use:

1. Sign up on Leonardo AI and access the dashboard.

2. Select the analysis or automation tools you need.

3. Configure the machine learning algorithms according to your specific requirements.

4. Monitor the results and optimize processes using the data provided by the platform.

## Google Colab

Google Colab is a free service that allows you to write and execute Python code directly in the browser, with no configuration required and free access to GPUs. It is widely used for the development and experimentation of machine learning models.

Key Features:

- Execution of Python code in the browser

- Free access to GPUs for training machine learning models

- Easy sharing of code notebooks

- Integration with Google Drive for file storage and management

How to Use:

1. Access Google Colab with your Google account.

2. Create a new notebook and start writing your Python code.

3. Use the available GPU resources to train machine learning models.

4. Save and share your notebooks with collaborators and colleagues.

## Microsoft CoPilot

Microsoft CoPilot is a virtual assistant integrated into Microsoft products like Office 365, using artificial intelligence to help users complete tasks more quickly and accurately.

Key Features:

- Intelligent suggestions for writing and editing documents
- Automation of repetitive tasks in Excel and other Office programs
- Integration with Microsoft Teams to enhance collaboration
- Data analysis and visualization tools

How to Use:

1. Access Office 365 and activate Microsoft CoPilot.
2. Use the intelligent suggestions while writing or editing documents.
3. Automate repetitive tasks in Excel with the help of CoPilot.
4. Collaborate with your team using CoPilot's integrations with Microsoft Teams.

## Dialogflow

Dialogflow, developed by Google, is a chatbot development platform that uses artificial intelligence to understand and respond to user requests. It is used to create natural and interactive conversational experiences across various communication channels.

Key Features:

- Creation of intelligent chatbots for various communication channels

- Natural Language Understanding (NLU)

- Integration with Google Assistant, Alexa, and other platforms

- Conversation analysis and optimization tools

How to Use:

1. Sign up for Dialogflow and create a new chatbot agent.

2. Define the chatbot's intents and responses using natural language.

3. Integrate the chatbot with the desired communication platforms.

4. Monitor conversations and optimize the chatbot based on interaction data.

## Google Bard

Google Bard is an artificial intelligence platform designed to create poetic and literary content. It uses advanced algorithms to generate texts that mimic specific literary styles, making it an interesting tool for writers and content creators.

Key Features:

- Generation of poetic and literary texts

- Support for different literary styles

- Text editing and customization tools

- Integration with publishing platforms

How to Use:

1. Access Google Bard and create a new writing project.

2. Choose the desired literary style and provide a starting prompt.

3. Use the editing tools to refine the generated text.

4. Export the text for publication or use in your creative projects.

## IBM Watson

IBM Watson is one of the most advanced and widely used artificial intelligence platforms at the enterprise level. It offers a wide range of services, including data analysis, machine learning, natural language processing, and more.

Key Features:

- Advanced data analysis

- Natural language processing

- Machine learning and deep learning

- Integration with various business services

How to Use:

1. Sign up on IBM Cloud and access IBM Watson.

2. Select the Watson services you need, such as data analysis or natural language processing.

3. Configure the services according to your specific needs.

4. Integrate Watson with your business workflows to optimize operations.

## Amazon Web Services (AWS) AI Services

AWS offers a comprehensive suite of artificial intelligence services, including Amazon SageMaker for machine learning, Amazon Rekognition for image analysis, and Amazon Polly for text-to-speech synthesis.

Key Features:

- Amazon SageMaker for developing and deploying machine learning models

- Amazon Rekognition for image and video recognition

- Amazon Polly for text-to-speech synthesis

- Wide range of analysis and automation tools

How to Use:

1. Access AWS and create an account.

2. Select the AI services you need, such as SageMaker or Rekognition.

3. Configure and train machine learning models using SageMaker.

4. Integrate AWS AI services into your projects to leverage AI capabilities.

## Azure AI

Azure AI, offered by Microsoft, includes services such as Azure Machine Learning, Cognitive Services, and Bot Service. These tools help create, train, and deploy artificial intelligence models at scale.

Key Features:

- Azure Machine Learning for developing machine learning models

- Cognitive Services for language, image, and video analysis

- Bot Service for developing intelligent chatbots

- Integration with other Azure services

How to Use:

1. Sign up for Microsoft Azure and access the dashboard.

2. Select the Azure AI services you need, such as Azure Machine Learning or Cognitive Services.

3. Configure and train machine learning models with Azure Machine Learning.

4. Use Cognitive Services to analyze complex data like text and images.

## H2O.ai

H2O.ai is an open-source platform that offers advanced tools for machine learning and artificial intelligence, including AutoML, data analysis, and visualization tools.

Key Features:

- AutoML to automate the machine learning process

- Data analysis and visualization tools

- Support for programming languages like R and Python

- Integration with cloud platforms like AWS and Azure

How to Use:

1. Download and install H2O.ai on your machine or use the cloud version.

2. Import your data and use AutoML to train machine learning models.

3. Analyze the results and visualize data using H2O.ai tools.

4. Integrate the trained models into your applications to enhance performance.

## Kensho

Kensho is an AI-based data analytics platform developed by S&P Global, designed to provide advanced financial analysis and forecasts.

Key Features:

- Predictive Analysis: Uses machine learning models to forecast market trends and financial behaviors.

- Natural Language Processing (NLP): Analyzes financial texts to extract relevant information.

- Data Visualization: Presents complex data clearly and comprehensively through interactive dashboards.

Advantages:

- Accuracy: Provides precise forecasts and detailed analyses based on historical and current data.

- Real-Time Updates: Continuously updates information to reflect the latest market conditions.

- Scalability: Easily adapts its functionalities to the needs of large financial institutions.

Applications:

- Investments / Risk management

- Financial research / Financial consulting

## 3.2 Artificial Intelligence Software

### ChatGPT

ChatGPT, developed by OpenAI, is a natural language model that can generate coherent and contextual text. It is used for various applications, including virtual assistants, content generation, customer support, and more.

Key Features:

- Generation of coherent and contextual text

- Understanding of natural language

- Integration with various applications

- Continuous learning capabilities

How to Use:

1. Sign up on OpenAI and access ChatGPT.

2. Integrate ChatGPT into your applications using the OpenAI API.

3. Configure the model to generate the desired types of text.

4. Use ChatGPT to enhance customer service, create content, or automate responses.

## ChatPDF

ChatPDF is an AI tool designed to analyze and interact with PDF documents. It allows extracting relevant information, creating summaries, and answering questions based on document content.

Key Features:

- Analysis and interpretation of PDF documents

- Extraction of relevant information

- Generation of summaries and answers to questions

- Integration with other document management tools

How to Use:

1. Upload a PDF document to ChatPDF.

2. Use the analysis features to extract specific information.

3. Generate summaries or answer questions based on the document's content.

4. Integrate ChatPDF with your workflows to improve document management efficiency.

## Synthesia

Synthesia is a platform that uses artificial intelligence to create videos with realistic avatars speaking in different languages. It is ideal for creating video content for marketing, training, and internal communications.

Key Features:

- Creation of realistic avatars

- Support for multiple languages

- Integration with video editing tools

- Ease of use for creating professional video content

How to Use:

1. Sign up on Synthesia and create an account.

2. Choose an avatar and customize the text and language of the video.

3. Generate the video and use editing tools to refine the content.

4. Export the video for use in your marketing, training, or internal communication projects.

## InVideo AI

InVideo AI is a video editing platform that utilizes artificial intelligence to simplify the process of creating and optimizing videos. It offers advanced tools to enhance video quality and automate the editing process.

Key Features:

- Automated video editing

- Video quality enhancement

- Automatic generation of subtitles and transcripts

- Wide range of templates and visual effects

How to Use:

1. Upload your video to InVideo AI.

2. Use the automated editing tools to improve video quality.

3. Add automatic subtitles and transcripts.

4. Export the optimized video for distribution on social media platforms or other channels.

## Flicky AI

Flicky AI is an artificial intelligence software designed for generating and editing video content. It uses advanced algorithms to improve video quality and automate complex editing processes.

Key Features:

- Video content generation and editing

- Video quality enhancement

- Automation of editing processes

- Integration with social media platforms

How to Use:

1. Access Flicky AI and upload your video.

2. Use the quality enhancement features to optimize the video.

3. Automate editing processes to save time and resources.

4. Share the optimized video on social media platforms or other channels.

## Descript

Descript is an audio and video editing platform that uses artificial intelligence to transcribe and edit content in a simple and intuitive manner. It is particularly useful for podcasters and video content creators.

Key Features:

- Automatic transcription of audio and video

- Text-based editing for audio and video

- Advanced voice recognition

- Integration with other content production tools

How to Use:

1. Upload your audio or video file to Descript.

2. Use the automatic transcription to generate text.

3. Edit the content using the text-based editor.

4. Export the final file for distribution.

## Tableau

Tableau is a data visualization tool that uses artificial intelligence to analyze and graphically represent complex data. It is widely used to create interactive dashboards and detailed reports.

Key Features:

- Advanced data visualization
- Creation of interactive dashboards
- Automated data analysis
- Integration with various data sources

How to Use:

1. Import your data into Tableau.
2. Use the visualization tools to create charts and dashboards.
3. Analyze the data using AI functionalities.
4. Share the dashboards and reports with your team or clients.

## Focus GitHub

Focus GitHub is a platform that uses artificial intelligence to help developers manage and optimize their projects on GitHub. It offers intelligent suggestions and automations to improve code efficiency.

Key Features:

- Intelligent code suggestions
- Automation of development workflows

- Integration with GitHub

- AI-based code analysis

How to Use:

1. Link your GitHub repository to Focus GitHub.

2. Use intelligent suggestions to improve your code.

3. Automate development workflows to increase efficiency.

4. Monitor project performance and make continuous optimizations.

## Freaky AI

Freaky AI is a software that leverages artificial intelligence to automate various business processes, from data management to content creation. It is designed to improve efficiency and reduce operational costs.

Key Features:

- Automation of business processes

- Advanced data management

- Automated content creation

- Integration with other business applications

How to Use:

1. Identify the business processes you want to automate with Freaky AI.

2. Configure the AI algorithms based on your specific needs.

3. Monitor and analyze the results to further optimize the processes.

4. Integrate Freaky AI with your business applications to maximize efficiency.

# D-ID

D-ID is a platform that uses artificial intelligence to create realistic videos from static images. It is used to create interactive and engaging multimedia content.

Key Features:

- Creation of realistic videos from static images
- Automatic generation of facial animations
- Integration with video editing tools
- Support for various input formats

How to Use:

1. Upload a static image to D-ID.

2. Configure the facial animations and other video settings.

3. Generate the video and use the editing tools to refine the content.

4. Export the video for use in your multimedia projects.

## Text-to-Speech AI Tools

Text-to-Speech (TTS) AI tools convert written text into spoken voice, providing solutions for creating voiceovers for videos, podcasts, and other audio content.

Key Features:

- Conversion of text into realistic speech

- Support for multiple languages and accents

- Customization of voice tone and pace

- Integration with audio editing tools

How to Use:

1. Select a TTS AI tool and create an account.

2. Upload or input the text you want to convert to speech.

3. Configure the voice settings, such as language and accent.

4. Generate the audio file and use it in your multimedia projects.

## Jasper AI

Jasper AI is one of the most advanced AI-assisted writing tools. It uses advanced language models to quickly and accurately generate high-quality content.

Features:

- Content Generation: Produces articles, blog posts, product descriptions, and other textual content with minimal input.

- Customization: Adapts the style and tone of the content based on user preferences.

- Collaboration: Allows multiple users to collaborate in real-time on writing projects.

Benefits:

- Efficiency: Significantly reduces the time needed to create written content.

- Quality: Generates coherent and grammatically correct content, improving overall writing quality.

- Flexibility: Supports various types of content, making it suitable for different marketing and communication needs.

Applications:

Blogging, copywriting, digital marketing, social media content creation.

## AlphaSense

AlphaSense is an AI-based search engine designed for businesses. It helps find and analyze financial and market information from a wide range of sources.

Features:

- Advanced Search: Enables in-depth searches in financial documents, transcripts, research articles, and other resources.

- Sentiment Analysis: Uses NLP to analyze text sentiment and help predict market trends.

- Custom Alerts: Notifies users of relevant changes and updates for their searches.

Benefits:

- Speed: Quickly finds relevant information, saving valuable time.

- Accuracy: Provides accurate and pertinent results through advanced search algorithms.

- Integration: Easily integrates with other analysis tools and platforms.

Applications:

Financial research, investment management, market analysis, strategic planning.

## Ahrefs

Ahrefs is one of the leading SEO and backlink analysis tools. It offers a comprehensive set of tools to improve online visibility and website performance.

Features:

- Backlink Analysis: Provides in-depth details on a site's backlinks, including competitors' backlinks.

- Keyword Research: Identifies high-potential keywords for content optimization.

- Site Audit: Scans websites to identify and resolve technical SEO issues.

- Rank Tracking: Monitors keyword rankings over time.

Benefits:

- Data Depth: Offers one of the most comprehensive backlink databases available.

- Accuracy: Provides precise and reliable SEO data to improve digital marketing strategy.

- Support and Community: Access to educational resources and an active support community.

Applications:

SEO, backlink analysis, keyword research, web content optimization.

## Lately.ai

Lately.ai is an AI-based content marketing platform that helps businesses create and distribute content on social media more efficiently. It uses AI to analyze existing content and generate new posts that resonate with the target audience.

Features:

- Content Generation: Analyzes long-form content like blogs or articles and transforms them into a series of social media posts.

- Performance Analysis: Provides insights on which types of content perform best and suggests improvements.

- Planning and Publishing: Automates the scheduling and publishing of posts across various social channels.

- Integration with Social Media Platforms: Integrates with platforms like Facebook, Twitter, LinkedIn, and others to streamline social media management.

Benefits:

- Efficiency: Saves time by automating the creation and publishing of social media content.

- Consistency: Ensures a constant social media presence with relevant and high-quality content.

- Data-Driven: Uses advanced analytics to continuously improve content strategies.

Applications:

Content marketing, social media management, brand management.

## AI Video Editing Platforms

These platforms use artificial intelligence to simplify and enhance the video editing process, offering advanced features such as automatic stabilization, facial recognition, and color correction.

Key Features:

- Automatic video stabilization

- Facial recognition and object tracking

- Color correction and video quality enhancement

- Integration with traditional video editing tools

How to Use:

1. Select an AI video editing platform and create an account.

2. Upload your video and use the automatic enhancement features.

3. Edit the video using the advanced tools offered by the platform.

4. Export the optimized video for distribution.

## CodePen

CodePen is an online platform that allows developers to write and share HTML, CSS, and JavaScript code. It is used to test and showcase development work in real-time.

Key Features:

- Writing and sharing HTML, CSS, and JavaScript code

- Real-time project preview

- Collaboration with other developers

- Integration with other development platforms

How to Use:

1. Create an account on CodePen and start a new project.

2. Write your HTML, CSS, and JavaScript code in your project.

3. View the real-time preview and make changes to the code.

4. Share the project with other developers or embed the code in your website.

## Tiny Host

Tiny Host is a platform that simplifies web hosting and development project management, offering AI tools for managing and optimizing web resources.

Key Features:

- Simplified hosting for websites and development projects

- Web resource management tools

- Automatic performance optimization

- Integration with development and design platforms

How to Use:

1. Create an account on Tiny Host and upload your web project.

2. Use the management tools to configure your website.

3. Optimize site performance using AI features.

4. Publish the website and monitor performance through Tiny Host's dashboard.

## Web Into App

Web Into App is a tool that allows you to transform websites into mobile applications using artificial intelligence, simplifying the app development process.

Key Features:

- Automatic conversion of websites into mobile apps
- Support for iOS and Android platforms
- Customization of app features
- Integration with web development tools

How to Use:

1. Create an account on Web Into App and upload your website.

2. Customize the app settings, such as layout and features.

3. Generate the mobile app and test it on supported devices.

4. Publish the app on app stores and monitor performance.

## Sudowrite

Sudowrite is a pioneer in the use of artificial intelligence for creative writing. Originally focused on creating articles, Sudowrite has recently expanded its capabilities with the release of Story Bible, making it a powerful tool for novel writing. It is particularly appreciated by authors for its ability to significantly speed up the writing process.

Features:

- Creative Writing: Assists in creating novels, short stories, and other creative content by providing AI-based text suggestions and completions.

- Story Bible: An advanced feature that helps authors plan and develop the plot, characters, and other narrative elements of the novel.

- Customized Packages: Offers packages like the Professional package, which is particularly useful for authors of long novels.

Advantages:

- Speed: Allows authors to write novels much faster than traditional methods.

- Creativity: Provides creative suggestions and helps overcome writer's block.

- Ease of Use: Intuitive and easy to use, even for those with no experience with AI tools.

Applications:

Novel writing, short stories, screenplays, and other creative projects.

## Claude

Claude is an AI developed by Anthropic, specializing in creating texts for novels. Many authors have found that Claude produces higher-quality narrative texts than ChatGPT. It has become a preferred tool for authors looking to improve the quality of their novels.

Features:

- Narrative Text Generation: Creates well-written and coherent texts for novels, offering high narrative quality.

- Customization: Allows authors to customize the tone, style, and themes of the generated texts to meet their specific needs.

- Creative Assistance: Provides suggestions and text completions, helping authors develop plots and characters.

Advantages:

- Text Quality: Produces high-quality narrative texts, often superior to those generated by other AIs like ChatGPT.

- Efficiency: Reduces the time needed to write novels while improving content quality.

- Creative Support: Helps overcome writer's block and stimulates new creative ideas.

Applications:

Novel writing, short stories, screenplays, and other creative projects.

# 3.3 Automation Tools

## Durabol

Durabol is an automation tool that uses artificial intelligence to optimize business processes, reducing the time and resources needed to complete repetitive tasks. It is particularly useful for small and medium-sized businesses looking to improve operational efficiency.

Key Features:

- Business process automation

- Reduction of task completion times

- Integration with various business systems

- Performance analysis of processes

How to Use:

1. Identify the business processes you want to automate with Durabol.

2. Configure the AI algorithms based on your specific needs.

3. Monitor and analyze the results to further optimize processes.

4. Integrate Durabol with your business systems to maximize efficiency.

## Fiverr

Fiverr is a freelance platform that uses artificial intelligence to match clients with the most suitable freelancers for their projects. It offers a wide range of services, from writing to programming, making it easy to find professionals for any type of project.

Key Features:

- Intelligent matching between clients and freelancers
- Wide range of available services
- Reviews and ratings of freelancers
- Project management tools

How to Use:

1. Sign up on Fiverr and create a profile.
2. Search for freelancers suitable for your project using advanced filters.
3. Contact freelancers and discuss project details.
4. Manage the project through the platform and monitor progress.

## Upwork

Upwork is a global freelance platform that leverages artificial intelligence to improve matchmaking between clients and professionals, ensuring higher efficiency and quality in completed projects.

Key Features:

- AI-based matchmaking algorithms

- Wide variety of job categories

- Project management tools

- Payment security and dispute resolution

How to Use:

1. Create an account on Upwork and complete your profile.

2. Post a project and specify the requirements.

3. Receive proposals from qualified freelancers and select the best candidate.

4. Use the project management tools to monitor progress and complete the work.

## Freelancer.com

Freelancer.com is another freelance platform that uses artificial intelligence algorithms to connect clients with freelancers, facilitating project management and collaboration.

Key Features:

- AI-based client and freelancer matching
- Project management and collaboration tools
- Payment security and dispute resolution
- Wide range of job categories

How to Use:

1. Sign up on Freelancer.com and create a profile.
2. Post a project with details and requirements.
3. Receive bids from freelancers and select the ideal candidate.
4. Manage the project through the platform and monitor progress.

## PromptBase

PromptBase is a platform that allows users to create and sell prompts for artificial intelligence, offering the ability to use these prompts to generate personalized content.

Key Features:

- Creation of AI prompts
- Marketplace for selling prompts
- Integration with various AI tools
- Community of users and prompt creators

How to Use:

1. Create an account on PromptBase and start creating custom prompts.

2. Publish your prompts on the marketplace and set a price.

3. Promote your prompts through the community and other channels.

4. Earn from the sales of your prompts and continue creating new ones.

## Adobe Firefly

Adobe Firefly is a graphic design tool that uses artificial intelligence to create customized images and graphics, enhancing designers' creativity and efficiency.

Key Features:

- Generation of custom images and graphics

- Advanced AI-based editing tools

- Integration with other Adobe software

- Extensive library of templates and graphic resources

How to Use:

1. Access Adobe Firefly through your Adobe account.

2. Choose a template or start a new design project.

3. Use AI-based editing tools to customize the graphics.

4. Export your creations for use in marketing, social media, and other channels.

## Adobe Stock and Shutterstock

Adobe Stock and Shutterstock are stock image platforms that use artificial intelligence to improve image search and management, offering more relevant and high-quality results.

Key Features:

- AI-based advanced search

- Extensive library of images, videos, and graphic resources

- Digital asset management tools

- Integration with design and editing software

How to Use:

1. Search for images or videos using AI-based advanced filters.

2. Purchase and download the necessary resources for your projects.

3. Use the images and videos in your design, marketing, and production projects.

4. Organize and manage your digital assets through the platform.

## RedBubble

RedBubble is a print-on-demand platform that uses artificial intelligence to match custom designs with a wide range of products, facilitating the sale of unique and creative items.

Key Features:

- Marketplace for selling customized products
- AI-based design tools
- Wide range of products available for printing
- Integration with other e-commerce platforms

How to Use:

1. Create an account on RedBubble and upload your designs.
2. Select the products you want to print your designs on.
3. Customize the products and set the price.
4. Promote your products through marketing channels and earn from sales.

## Canva

Canva is a graphic design tool that uses artificial intelligence to simplify the creation of professional graphics, offering customizable templates and intuitive tools.

Key Features:

- Extensive library of templates and graphic resources
- AI-based design tools

- Integration with social media and marketing platforms

- Ease of use for users of all levels

How to Use:

1. Access Canva and choose a design template.

2. Customize the design using the available editing tools.

3. Export the design for use in your marketing, social media, and other projects.

4. Share the design directly on social media platforms or via email.

## Printify

Printify is a print-on-demand platform that uses artificial intelligence to manage the production and distribution of customized products, facilitating the creation and sale of unique items.

Key Features:

- Creation and sale of customized products

- Automated management of production and distribution

- Wide range of available products

- Integration with e-commerce platforms

How to Use:

1. Create an account on Printify and upload your designs.

2. Select the products you want to print your designs on.

3. Customize the products and sync them with your e-commerce store.

4. Manage orders and monitor sales through the Printify dashboard.

## Etsy

Etsy is an e-commerce platform that uses artificial intelligence to enhance product discovery and matching between buyers and sellers, facilitating the sale of handmade and personalized items.

Key Features:

- Marketplace for selling handmade and personalized products

- Marketing and store management tools

- Integration with AI tools for product discovery

- Community of buyers and sellers

How to Use:

1. Create an account on Etsy and set up your shop.

2. Upload your products and customize the listings.

3. Use marketing tools to promote your products.

4. Manage orders and customer communications through the platform.

## Kittle

Kittle is a graphic design tool that uses artificial intelligence to create logos, graphics, and other customized visual elements, enhancing design efficiency and quality.

Key Features:

- Creation of custom logos and graphics
- AI-based design tools
- Extensive library of templates and graphic resources
- Ease of use for designers of all levels

How to Use:

1. Access Kittle and choose a design template.
2. Customize the design using AI-based editing tools.
3. Export the design for use in your branding and marketing projects.
4. Share the design directly on social media platforms or via email.

# EverBee

EverBee is a market analysis tool that uses artificial intelligence to identify trends and business opportunities, helping companies make informed and strategic decisions.

Key Features:

- AI-based market analysis
- Identification of trends and business opportunities
- Data visualization tools
- Integration with e-commerce and marketing platforms

How to Use:

1. Access EverBee and create an account.
2. Import your market data or use the data provided by the platform.
3. Analyze trends and identify business opportunities.
4. Use the insights to make strategic decisions and improve business performance.

# Zapier

Zapier is an automation platform that allows you to connect different applications and services using artificial intelligence, automating workflows and improving operational efficiency.

Key Features:

- Workflow automation
- Integration with over 2000 applications

- Customizable triggers and actions

- Ease of use for users of all levels

How to Use:

1. Create an account on Zapier and select the applications you want to connect.

2. Configure the triggers and actions to automate your workflows.

3. Test the automations to ensure they work correctly.

4. Monitor and optimize the automations to improve operational efficiency.

## Microsoft Power Automate

Microsoft Power Automate is a business process automation tool that allows you to create automated workflows between applications and services.

Key Features:

- Creation of automated workflows

- Integration with Microsoft and third-party applications

- Event-based triggers

- Analysis and monitoring of workflow performance

How to Use:

1. Access Microsoft Power Automate through your Microsoft account.

2. Create a new workflow and select the applications to connect.

3. Configure the triggers and actions to automate processes.

4. Monitor and optimize workflows through the Power Automate dashboard.

## IFTTT (If This Then That)

IFTTT is an automation platform that allows you to create simple chains of conditions, called applets, to automate tasks between different applications and devices.

Key Features:

- Creation of applets for task automation
- Integration with over 600 services
- Ease of use for non-technical users
- User community for sharing applets

How to Use:

1. Create an account on IFTTT and explore the available applets.

2. Select an existing applet or create a new one.

3. Configure the triggers and actions to automate tasks.

4. Activate the applet and monitor the automated tasks.

## SEMrush

SEMrush is a digital marketing platform that offers tools for search engine optimization (SEO), competitor analysis, and advertising campaign management.

Features:

- SEO: Provides keyword analysis, site audit, and recommendations to improve search engine rankings.

- Keyword Research: Identifies the best keywords to target for increasing online visibility.

- Competitor Analysis: Offers detailed insights into competitors' SEO and marketing strategies.

- PPC Campaign Management: Optimizes pay-per-click (PPC) campaigns on Google Ads and other advertising networks.

Benefits:

- Comprehensive: Offers a wide range of tools in a single platform, making it easy to manage various aspects of digital marketing.

- Data-Driven: Uses detailed and up-to-date data to inform marketing decisions.

- User-Friendly: Has an intuitive interface that makes even advanced features accessible.

Applications:

SEO, digital marketing, online advertising, market research.

# MetaTrader

MetaTrader is a widely used electronic trading platform for forex, futures, options, and other financial instruments. MetaTrader 4 (MT4) and MetaTrader 5 (MT5) offer powerful features for technical analysis and automated trading.

Features:

- Automated Trading: Allows users to create, test, and implement automated trading strategies through Expert Advisors (EA).

- Technical Analysis: Provides a wide range of technical analysis tools, including customizable indicators, advanced charts, and drawing tools.

- Multi-platform Trading: Supports trading on desktop, web, and mobile devices, offering flexibility and continuous market access.

- MetaTrader Marketplace: Provides access to a vast library of trading tools, indicators, and EAs created by third-party developers.

- Notifications and Alerts: Enables users to set custom alerts for specific market events or price changes.

Benefits:

- Flexibility: Suitable for both manual traders and those who prefer automated trading.

- Community and Support: Strong community support and plenty of educational resources to help users maximize the platform's capabilities.

- Advanced Tools: Offers advanced risk management and technical analysis tools to help traders make more informed decisions.

Applications:

Forex trading, futures trading, portfolio management, technical analysis, automated trading strategy development.

## Otter.ai

Otter.ai is an AI-powered tool designed for automatic transcription and voice note management. It is widely used for recording and transcribing meetings, interviews, lectures, and other forms of spoken communication.

Features:

- Automatic Transcription: Records and transcribes conversations in real-time with high accuracy.

- Collaboration: Allows users to share transcripts and collaborate by adding comments and edits.

- Note Organization: Enables organizing transcripts into folders and searching for specific keywords within the transcribed texts.

- Platform Integration: Integrates with videoconferencing tools like Zoom, Microsoft Teams, and Google Meet, facilitating the recording and transcription of meetings.

- Intelligent Summarization: Generates summaries of conversations and identifies key points.

Benefits:

- Efficiency: Automates the transcription process, saving time and resources.

- Accuracy: Provides accurate transcriptions thanks to advanced speech recognition algorithms.

- Accessibility: Facilitates access to and review of conversations, enhancing productivity and collaboration.

Applications:

Meeting transcription, voice note management, creation of text documents from audio, accessibility support.

# 3.4 Social and Content Platforms

## Opus Clip

Opus Clip is a tool that uses artificial intelligence to create and edit video clips for social media, optimizing content for greater visibility and engagement. It is particularly useful for marketers and content creators looking to maximize the impact of their videos on social media.

Key Features:

- Automatic creation of video clips

- Content optimization for social media

- Video performance analysis

- Integration with various social media platforms

How to Use:

1. Upload your video to Opus Clip.

2. Use the editing tools to create optimized clips.

3. Analyze the performance of the clips through the dashboard.

4. Share the clips on your social media channels to maximize engagement.

## YouTube

YouTube is a video-sharing platform that uses artificial intelligence to suggest content, optimize searches, and analyze video performance. It is essential for content creators who want to reach a wide audience.

Key Features:

- AI-based content suggestions

- Video search optimization

- Performance analysis tools

- Content monetization

How to Use:

1. Create a YouTube channel and upload your videos.

2. Use the optimization tools to improve your video visibility.

3. Analyze video performance through YouTube Analytics.

4. Monetize your videos through advertisements and sponsorships.

## YouTube Shorts

YouTube Shorts is a feature of YouTube that allows users to create and share short videos. It uses artificial intelligence to optimize content visibility and engagement.

Key Features:

- Creation of short videos

- AI-based optimization

- Video performance analysis

- Integration with the main YouTube channel

How to Use:

1. Create short videos using the YouTube app.

2. Optimize the videos to increase visibility and engagement.

3. Analyze video performance through YouTube Analytics.

4. Integrate Shorts with your main YouTube channel to maximize impact.

## TikTok

TikTok is a social media platform that uses artificial intelligence to personalize users' feeds by suggesting relevant and engaging content. It is ideal for content creators who want to reach a young and dynamic audience.

Key Features:

- AI-based feed personalization
- Video creation and editing tools
- Content performance analysis
- Monetization opportunities through sponsorships and partnerships

How to Use:

1. Create a TikTok account and start creating video content.
2. Use the editing tools to enhance the quality of your videos.
3. Analyze your content performance through TikTok Analytics.
4. Monetize your content through collaborations and sponsorships.

## Instagram

Instagram is a social media platform that uses artificial intelligence to enhance content discovery, suggest posts, and analyze user engagement. It is essential for brands and visual content creators.

Key Features:

- AI-based content suggestions
- Photo and video creation and editing tools
- Post performance analysis
- Monetization opportunities through ads and collaborations

How to Use:

1. Create an Instagram account and publish high-quality visual content.
2. Use the editing tools to enhance your posts.
3. Analyze your content performance through Instagram Insights.
4. Monetize your posts through brand collaborations and advertising.

## Instagram Reels

Instagram Reels is a feature on Instagram that allows users to create and share short videos. It uses artificial intelligence to optimize content visibility and engagement.

Key Features:

- Creation of short videos

- AI-based optimization

- Video performance analysis

- Integration with the main Instagram profile

How to Use:

1. Create short videos using the Instagram Reels feature.

2. Optimize the videos to increase visibility and engagement.

3. Analyze video performance through Instagram Insights.

4. Integrate Reels with your main Instagram profile to maximize impact.

## LinkedIn

LinkedIn is a professional networking platform that uses artificial intelligence to suggest connections, analyze profiles, and enhance content discovery. It is ideal for professionals and businesses looking to expand their network and promote their services.

Key Features:

- AI-based connection suggestions

- Profile analysis tools

- Professional content optimization

- Advertising and lead generation opportunities

How to Use:

1. Create a complete and professional LinkedIn profile.

2. Connect with relevant professionals and companies.

3. Post professional content and use LinkedIn Analytics to analyze performance.

4. Use LinkedIn Ads to promote your services and generate leads.

## YouTube Studio

YouTube Studio is a tool for managing YouTube channels that uses artificial intelligence to analyze video performance, suggest optimizations, and improve content management.

Key Features:

- Video performance analysis
- AI-based optimization suggestions
- Content management tools
- Revenue and interaction monitoring

How to Use:

1. Access YouTube Studio through your YouTube account.

2. Analyze your video performance using the analysis tools.

3. Follow optimization suggestions to improve your content.

4. Manage your channel and monitor revenue and interactions.

## Pinterest

Pinterest is a visual discovery platform that uses artificial intelligence to suggest content based on user interests. It is ideal for brands and content creators looking to reach an audience interested in visual ideas and inspiration.

Key Features:

- AI-based content suggestions
- Pin creation and sharing tools
- Pin performance analysis
- Advertising and promotion opportunities

How to Use:

1. Create a Pinterest account and start creating visually appealing pins.
2. Use the creation tools to enhance your pins.
3. Analyze your pin performance through Pinterest Analytics.
4. Promote your pins through Pinterest Ads to increase visibility.

# Medium

Medium is a blogging platform that uses artificial intelligence to suggest articles and enhance content discovery. It is ideal for writers and bloggers looking to share their ideas and reach a wider audience.

Key Features:

- AI-based article suggestions

- Article creation and publishing tools

- Article performance analysis

- Monetization opportunities through the partner program

How to Use:

1. Create a Medium account and start writing articles.

2. Use the creation tools to improve the quality of your articles.

3. Publish your articles and analyze performance through Medium Analytics.

4. Monetize your articles by joining the Medium partner program.

# Chapter 4: Creating Income Streams and Online Opportunities with AI

Artificial intelligence (AI) is rapidly becoming a driving force in numerous sectors, offering tools and technologies that not only improve operational efficiency but also open new avenues for generating passive income. In this chapter, we will explore how AI can be leveraged to create consistent and automated income streams, reducing the need for continuous human intervention. Whether you are an emerging entrepreneur, a technology professional, or simply curious about new earning opportunities, you will find practical strategies and concrete examples in these pages on how to use AI to your advantage.

## 4.1 Creating Digital Content

We will start with digital content creation, an area where AI can make a big difference. From automated writing to generating videos and images, AI tools can help you produce high-quality content quickly and efficiently. You will discover how to automate self-publishing, create viral videos, and manage a blog without spending hours writing and editing.

## 4.2 Design and Digital Art

Design and digital art represent another promising area for passive income thanks to AI. Advanced AI-assisted design tools can generate logos, illustrations, social media graphics, and even digital art that can be sold as NFTs. We will explore how these tools can be used to create personalized products, sell stock images, and produce digital art.

## 4.3 Development and Programming

Programming and application development have traditionally been labor-intensive activities, but AI is changing this sector as well. You will discover how to create and sell smartphone apps using AI tools that simplify the development process. From developing chatbots to automating business processes, we will see how AI can be used to build innovative software solutions.

## 4.4 Analysis and Consulting

Data analysis and strategic consulting are fundamental to the success of many businesses. AI offers powerful analytical tools that can transform large volumes of data into useful insights. This section will guide you through the use of interactive dashboards, automated SEO consulting, and data-driven content generation. You will discover how to offer AI-based consulting services that can help companies make more informed and strategic decisions.

## 4.5 Marketing and Sales

Marketing and sales are areas where AI can truly make a difference. From optimizing advertising campaigns to creating social media content, AI tools can significantly enhance the effectiveness of your marketing initiatives. We will explore how to create and sell prompts, manage automated advertising campaigns, and use AI to generate engaging content that attracts and retains customers.

## 4.6 Other Opportunities

Finally, we will explore other passive income opportunities offered by AI. From automated trading to creating virtual influencers, to automating business processes and providing automated translation services, we will see how AI can be applied in innovative ways to generate income. These activities demonstrate how AI can be used to optimize and automate complex tasks, allowing you to focus your energies on more strategic activities.

## 4.1 Creating Digital Content

Let's start exploring the various activities that can be automated or optimized with AI, allowing you to earn money continuously with minimal intervention. Discover how AI can transform your approach to digital content creation, enhancing the quality of your content and reducing the time required to produce engaging and profitable materials. This way, you'll have more time to dedicate to your professional development, studying new projects that guarantee additional income, or simply enjoying more time for yourself, your family, or your hobbies.

## Self-Publishing with AI

Self-publishing is an excellent way to create a passive income stream. Thanks to artificial intelligence, many stages of the publishing process can be automated, from writing and editing to formatting and book promotion.

### How to Proceed:

1. Writing and Editing: Use ChatGPT to write and edit your manuscript. For example, you can start by providing ChatGPT with a brief summary of the chapter and let it develop further. This allows you to produce consistent and high-quality content in less time.

2. Formatting and Publishing: Once the manuscript is complete, you can use self-publishing tools like Amazon's Kindle Direct Publishing (KDP). KDP offers an intuitive interface for uploading your book, setting the price, and publishing it in eBook or paperback format.

3. Promotion: Promotion is crucial for your book's success. Use automated digital marketing strategies, such as advertising campaigns on Amazon Advertising, and leverage social platforms to reach a wider audience.

### Practical Example

Suppose you want to write a science fiction novel. Start by asking ChatGPT to develop a plot based on your basic idea. Once you have a draft, continue interacting with ChatGPT to enrich the details and create chapters. After completing the manuscript, proceed with formatting and creating the cover, upload it to KDP, set the price, and start promoting it.

## Video Content Creation and YouTube

YouTube is one of the most profitable platforms for creating video content. Artificial intelligence can help produce high-quality videos with minimal effort. Tools like InVideo AI and Synthesia enable you to create engaging videos without investing in expensive equipment or editing software.

## How to Proceed:

1. Content Planning: Plan your video content using ChatGPT to generate interesting scripts. For example, you can ask ChatGPT to develop a script for a tutorial or a product review.

2. Video Creation: Use Synthesia to create videos using realistic avatars. This tool allows you to produce professional videos without the need for a film crew.

3. Editing and Optimization: Use InVideo AI to add visual effects, transitions, and subtitles. This makes the video more engaging and professional.

4. Publishing and Promotion: Upload the video to YouTube and optimize it for SEO using YouTube Studio. Make sure to use relevant keywords and promote the video on social media to maximize visibility.

## Practical Example

If you want to create a tech product review channel, start by asking ChatGPT to generate a script for reviewing a new smartphone. Use Synthesia to create the video, adding effects and transitions with InVideo AI. Finally, publish the video on YouTube and use YouTube Studio to optimize its visibility.

## Creating and Monetizing Viral Content with AI

Creating viral content on social media can generate significant passive income. AI can help you identify trends and create content that resonates with your audience. Tools like Opus Clip and TikTok can be used to produce and distribute engaging content.

## How to Proceed:

1. Trend Analysis: Analyze current trends using TikTok Analytics. This will help you understand what is popular and create content that aligns with these trends.

2. Content Creation: Use Opus Clip to create short, engaging videos that can easily go viral. For example, you can create challenge videos, tutorials, or comedic sketches.

3. Distribution and Promotion: Publish your content on TikTok and other social platforms. Engage with the audience to increase interaction and use relevant hashtags to reach a wider audience.

## Practical Example

If you notice a new challenge becoming viral on TikTok, use Opus Clip to create your version of the challenge. Publish the video and promote it through your social channels to increase visibility and engagement.

## Copywriting and Content Creation Services

Offering copywriting services can be a great source of passive income, especially when automated with AI. Jasper AI is a powerful tool that can generate articles, blog posts, product descriptions, and more with minimal intervention.

## How to Proceed:

1. Content Generation: Set up Jasper AI to generate high-quality content on various topics. For example, you can ask Jasper AI to write an article on digital marketing or a detailed product description.

2. Service Offering: Create a website or use freelance platforms like Fiverr and Upwork to offer your services. Publish examples of previous work and clearly describe what your service packages include. If you don't have previous work examples, create sample works specifically to showcase your skills and strengths.

3. Automation and Client Management: Use Zapier to automate the process of acquiring and managing clients. For example, you can automate responses to inquiries and invoice sending.

### Practical Example

If a client asks you to write a series of articles for their blog, use Jasper AI to quickly generate high-quality content, which you then review, enhance, and expand. Publish these articles on the client's blog and automate the management of revisions and communications through Zapier.

## Automated Blogging

Blogging is another activity that can generate passive income. With AI, you can automate the creation and publishing of articles on niche topics. Tools like ChatGPT for writing and WordPress for blog management make this process simple and efficient.

### How to Proceed:

1. Content Creation: Use ChatGPT to generate articles on specific topics. For example, you can ask ChatGPT to

help you write an article on a trending topic in your industry.

2. Blog Management: Set up a blog on WordPress and use plugins for SEO and performance analysis. Schedule automatic publication of articles according to an editorial calendar.

3. Monetization: Monetize the blog through ads, affiliate links, and digital product sales. Use marketing tools to promote your blog and increase traffic.

### Practical Example

If you have a travel blog, use ChatGPT to help you generate articles on popular destinations. Set up WordPress to automatically publish these articles weekly and integrate Google AdSense to earn from ad views.

## Utilizing AI Voice Synthesis Tools

Voiceovers are a key component for many digital contents. AI voice synthesis tools, such as those offered by Descript, can create realistic voiceovers for videos, podcasts, and advertisements.

### How to Proceed:

1. Script Creation: Write the voiceover script using ChatGPT. For example, you can ask ChatGPT to create a script for a promotional video or a podcast episode.

2. Voiceover Generation: Use Descript to convert the text into speech. Descript offers various synthetic voices that can be customized to match the tone of the content.

3. Integration into Content: Integrate the voiceover into your videos or podcasts using editing software like Adobe Premiere or Audacity.

## Practical Example

If you are creating a promotional video for a product, use ChatGPT to write an engaging script. Generate the voiceover with Descript and integrate it into the video using Adobe Premiere. This allows you to create high-quality content in less time and with less effort.

We have seen how artificial intelligence offers powerful tools for creating high-quality digital content with minimal intervention. By leveraging these technologies, you can generate passive income through various activities, from publishing books to creating viral videos and managing automated blogs. Now, let's continue to explore further opportunities to diversify your income streams using AI.

## Writing a Novel Using Artificial Intelligence Tools

If you're not using artificial intelligence to help you write, you might be falling behind. AI has made significant strides in a short time and is one of the best ways to help writers take their books from draft to publication as quickly as possible. Despite many online trolls discouraging authors from using AI software as an aid, do readers really care if AI assisted in the process, as long as the novel is well-written, engaging, and captivating?

Here's how you can use some AI tools to write a novel or at least overcome your writer's block.

## AI Tools for Writers

Currently, there are three main tools that authors rely on when creating content for their novels:

- Sudowrite: The primary writing tool.
- ChatGPT: Ideal for generating ideas and short paragraphs.
- Claude: Useful for ideas and brief paragraphs.

### How to Proceed

1. Story Ideas Whether you have an initial idea to start from or you're navigating completely blind, AI tools are unparalleled in this task. You can ask AI tools to generate ideas for plots, characters, and settings.

2. Chapter Outlines In writing, there are "plotters" and "pantsers." Plotters meticulously plan every part of their story before they start writing, while pantsers make it up as they go. You can use AI for both types of writers. To start, simply ask the AI to create a chapter outline.

3. Writing a Novel Currently, you can't ask an AI tool to write an entire bestselling novel and have it generated on the spot. However, you can use AI tools to write complete chapters and scenes, then stitch them together to create your novel. AI tools like Sudowrite, ChatGPT, and Claude can help you create coherent and well-structured content.

4. Editing Editing your book helps you find parts where your story doesn't flow well or may be confusing, while proofreading helps you correct grammatical and spelling errors. You don't need to spend money to correct many of these types of errors, as most writing tools include some form of spell-check and grammar tools.

## Balancing AI and Human Input

While AI tools are powerful aids, it's important to find a balance between their assistance and your unique style. Use them as a tool to enhance your writing process, but ensure that your novel still reflects your unique voice. A human touch is essential to build a world that resonates with your readers.

# 4.2 Design and Digital Art

Artificial intelligence is transforming the world of design and digital art, making it possible to create unique and personalized works with minimal human intervention. This revolution not only democratizes access to creative tools but also offers new opportunities to generate passive income. In this part of the book, we will explore various design and digital art activities that can be enhanced by AI, using the tools and platforms described in the previous chapter.

## Creating Custom Graphics and Images

The creation of custom graphics and images is a continuously growing sector. Using AI tools like Adobe Firefly and MidJourney, you can generate logos, digital art, smartphone covers, stickers, and much more. These tools allow you to create unique designs that can be sold on various e-commerce platforms.

### Steps to Get Started:

1. Creating Designs:

   - Use Adobe Firefly to start creating unique designs. Firefly offers intuitive AI-based tools to generate personalized images.

   - Alternatively, explore MidJourney to create digital artwork with a more pronounced artistic touch. MidJourney allows you to generate images from detailed textual descriptions.

2. Preparing Products:

   - Once you have created your designs, access print-on-demand platforms like Printify, Teespring, or RedBubble.

   - Upload your designs onto various available products such as t-shirts, mugs, posters, smartphone covers, and more.

3. Customization and Optimization:

   - Customize the products with options for color, size, and style.

   - Write engaging descriptions and use relevant keywords to improve the visibility of your products in searches.

4. Promotion and Sales:

- Promote your products through social media, email marketing campaigns, and collaborations with influencers.

- Use platforms like Instagram and Pinterest to showcase your designs and attract a wider audience.

5. Managing Sales:

- Print-on-demand platforms handle production, shipping, and customer service, allowing you to focus on creating new designs and promoting them.

Selling custom graphics and images on print-on-demand platforms allows you to earn a commission on each sale without directly managing production or shipping.

## Selling Stock Images on Stock Photo Platforms

Stock photo platforms like Adobe Stock and Shutterstock are constantly seeking new high-quality images. Using AI tools, you can create and upload images that meet the needs of these platforms, generating passive income through sales.

### How to Proceed:

1. Creating Images:

- Use DALL-E or MidJourney to create high-quality images that are visually appealing and match current market trends.

2. Preparing for Upload:

- Edit and optimize the images using editing software like Adobe Photoshop or Canva to ensure they are ready for sale.

- Save the images in high-resolution formats with relevant file names.

3. Uploading to Platforms:

  - Create accounts on Adobe Stock and Shutterstock.

  - Upload the images and add detailed descriptions, titles, and tags to enhance their visibility in searches.

4. Content Optimization:

  - Monitor the performance of your images through the dashboards on Adobe Stock and Shutterstock.

  - Regularly update your images and add new content to keep customer interest high.

5. Monetization:

  - Each time someone purchases or downloads one of your images, you receive a commission.

  - Maintain a diverse collection of images to attract a wider audience and increase sales.

## Creating and Selling Digital Art as NFTs

Blockchain technology has opened new opportunities for digital artists through the sale of NFTs (Non-Fungible Tokens). Tools like Leonardo AI and DALL-E can help you create unique artworks that can be sold as NFTs on platforms like OpenSea.

### Step-by-Step Guide:

1. Creating Artworks:

  - Use Leonardo AI or DALL-E to create unique digital artworks. These tools allow you to generate complex and original images with minimal human intervention.

2.  Preparing for Minting:

    - Save your artworks in formats compatible with NFT platforms.

    - Add details such as the title, description, and technical specifications of the artwork.

3.  Minting NFTs:

    - Create a cryptocurrency wallet on platforms like MetaMask.

    - Connect your wallet to OpenSea or other NFT platforms.

    - Upload your artworks and follow the instructions to mint your NFTs.

4.  Promoting Your Artworks:

    - Use social media, blogs, and forums dedicated to crypto art to promote your works.

    - Participate in NFT artist communities to increase visibility and sales.

5.  Monetization:

    - When someone purchases your NFT, you receive a payment in cryptocurrency.

    - Some platforms allow you to earn a percentage on future sales of your NFT, generating additional passive income.

## Creating Logos and Designs for Businesses

Many small businesses and startups are looking for attractive logos and designs for their branding. Using design tools like

Canva and Adobe Firefly, you can create high-quality logos and graphics that can be sold directly to clients or through freelance platforms like Fiverr and Upwork.

**Tips for Success:**

1. Creating Designs:

   - Use Canva to create logos and other branding elements. Canva offers a wide range of customizable templates and intuitive design tools.

   - Leverage Adobe Firefly to create more complex and personalized designs.

2. Offering Services:

   - Create a profile on freelance platforms like Fiverr and Upwork.

   - Post your service offerings, specifying what your design packages include (logos, business cards, social media graphics).

3. Client Management:

   - Respond promptly to client inquiries and offer revisions to ensure their satisfaction.

   - Use project management tools like Trello or Asana to keep track of deadlines and tasks.

4. Monetization:

   - Earn by offering complete branding packages.

   - Use client reviews to build your reputation and attract new clients.

## Selling Customized Products on Print on Demand Platforms

Platforms like RedBubble, Teespring, and Printify allow you to upload your designs and sell them on a wide range of products, from clothing to home accessories. AI can help you create appealing designs that resonate with your audience.

**How to Proceed:**

1. Creating Designs:

   - Use Adobe Firefly to create unique and visually appealing designs.

   - Experiment with Canva to add text, filters, and other graphic elements, making the product more personalized and original.

2. Preparing Products:

   - Upload your designs to print on demand platforms like RedBubble, Teespring, and Printify.

   - Select the products you want to print your designs on and customize them.

3. Publishing and Promotion:

   - Publish your products in the online stores of the platforms.

   - Promote your products through social media campaigns, email marketing, and collaborations with influencers.

4. Managing Sales:

   - Print on demand platforms handle production, shipping, and customer service, allowing you to focus on creating and promoting designs.

   - Monitor sales and customer reviews to optimize your products and adjust your marketing strategies.

## Creating and Selling Custom Tarot Decks

A niche but growing market is that of custom tarot decks. Using AI tools to create unique, original, or personalized designs, you can sell tarot decks on platforms like Printify and Etsy.

### Steps to Get Started:

1. Creating Designs:

    - Design the tarot cards using MidJourney. This tool allows you to create detailed and unique designs for each card in the deck.

2. Customizing the Cards:

    - Add extraordinary and meaningful details to each card, making them special and distinctive.

    - Use Adobe Firefly to refine the designs and add graphic elements.

3. Preparing Products:

    - Upload the designs to Printify to create custom tarot decks.

    - Configure product details such as card type, packaging, and other customization options.

4. Selling and Promotion:

    - Open a store on Etsy and publish your tarot decks.

    - Promote your products through social media, niche blogs, and tarot enthusiast communities.

5. Managing Sales:

    - Manage orders and customer interactions through Etsy.

- Provide excellent customer service to build a loyal customer base.

We have seen how AI makes it possible to create unique works and monetize them through various platforms, from logos and graphics to stock images and NFT art. With strategic use of these tools, you can turn your creativity into a constant source of income.

# 4.3 Development and Programming

The field of development and programming has also experienced significant disruption with the advent of artificial intelligence. AI offers advanced tools that can automate complex tasks and improve the efficiency of development processes. In this part of the book, we will explore various development and programming activities that can generate passive income through the use of AI. We will utilize tools and platforms described in previous chapters to show how to best leverage these opportunities.


## Website Creation

Creating websites is one of the most in-demand activities in the development field. With the help of AI tools, it is possible to create and optimize websites quickly and efficiently. Platforms like Tenweb.io and Google Colab make this process much simpler, allowing you to offer quality website creation services to a wide range of clients.

### Steps to Get Started:

1. Website Planning:
   - Collaborate with the client, organizing meetings or work calls to understand their needs and goals. This phase must be conducted in synergy with the

client because the more information, details, and understanding you have about their desires and expectations, the better you can work to satisfy them.

- Use Tenweb.io to choose a suitable template and then customize it according to the client's specifications, making communication with the client in the initial phase critical.

2. Development and Customization:

   - Use Tenweb.io's tools to create the website, leveraging AI-assisted design features to enhance aesthetics and functionality.

   - If necessary, use Google Colab to develop custom features, writing and testing code directly in the browser with access to GPUs for machine learning tasks.

3. SEO Optimization:

   - Integrate SEO plugins and analysis tools to optimize the site for search engines.

   - Use AI to analyze content and improve keywords and site structure.

4. Launch and Monitoring:

   - Publish the site and monitor its performance using analysis tools like Google Analytics.

   - Offer maintenance and update services to ensure the site remains optimized and secure.

5. Monetization:

   - Invoice clients for website development and customization services.

   - Offer maintenance and update packages to generate recurring revenue.

## Development of AI Chatbots and Automation

Chatbots and AI automation are powerful tools for enhancing customer interaction and automating repetitive processes. Platforms like Dialogflow and Microsoft Bot Framework allow for the development of customized chatbots for various purposes, from websites to e-commerce platforms.

### How to Proceed:

1. Defining Chatbot Objectives:

   - Identify Tasks: Determine the tasks the chatbot should perform (e.g., answering frequently asked questions, customer support, booking appointments).

   - Plan Conversation Flow: Outline the conversation flow and responses the chatbot should provide.

2. Developing the Chatbot:

   - Create and Train: Use Dialogflow to create and train the chatbot, defining intents and corresponding responses.

   - Integration: Integrate the chatbot with desired platforms, such as websites, Facebook Messenger, or other messaging applications.

3. Customization and Testing:

   - Behavior and Appearance: Customize the chatbot's behavior and appearance using design tools.

   - Testing: Test the chatbot to ensure it responds correctly to a wide range of questions and scenarios.

4. Implementation and Monitoring:

- Deploy: Implement the chatbot on the website or e-commerce platform.

- Monitor: Use analytics tools to monitor interactions and optimize the chatbot's responses.

5. Monetization:

- Service Offering: Offer chatbot development services to small and medium-sized businesses.

- Maintenance Packages: Provide maintenance and update packages to ensure the chatbot remains effective and up-to-date.

## Creating and Selling a Smartphone App

Developing smartphone apps can be a lucrative source of passive income, especially when automated with AI. With tools like ChatGPT, CodePen, and conversion platforms like Web Into App, it is possible to develop apps without complex coding. Below is a detailed guide on how to create and sell a smartphone app using ChatGPT.

Steps to Create a Smartphone App Using ChatGPT

### 1. Define the App Idea

Tool: ChatGPT

Steps:

- Describe the App: Start by explaining to ChatGPT the type of app you want to create. For example, you can say, "I want to create a to-do list app that allows users to add, view, and complete tasks."

- Use Examples: Use an example app, like a to-do list, to facilitate ChatGPT's understanding. This will help generate more precise and useful suggestions.

## 2. Generate the HTML Code

Tool: ChatGPT

Steps:

- Request HTML: Ask ChatGPT to generate the HTML code for the app. For example, "Generate the HTML code for a section that allows users to add new tasks, one to view pending tasks, and one for completed tasks."

- Specify Sections: Ensure ChatGPT understands each part of the app you want to create by specifying the necessary sections.

## 3. Generate the CSS Code

Tool: ChatGPT

Steps:

- Request CSS: Ask ChatGPT to generate the CSS code for the app. For example, "Generate the CSS code with an aqua background and modern styles for buttons and lists."

- Aesthetic Preferences: Specify aesthetic preferences, such as colors, fonts, and layout.

### 4. Generate the JavaScript Code

Tool: ChatGPT

Steps:

- Request JavaScript: Ask ChatGPT to generate the JavaScript code necessary for the app's functionality. For example, "Generate the JavaScript code to add new tasks to the list, move them to the completed section, and delete them."

- Functionality Reminder: Remind ChatGPT of the app's functionality to ensure all features are included in the code.

### 5. Verify the Code on CodePen

Tool: CodePen

Steps:

- Paste the Code: Copy and paste the HTML, CSS, and JavaScript code generated by ChatGPT into CodePen.

- Verify Functionality: Ensure that the app functions correctly. Make sure all features are operational and the design meets your expectations.

### 6. Save the Code Files on Your PC

Steps:

- Create a Folder: Create a new folder on your desktop to organize the app's files.

- Save the Files: Save the code files (index.html, styles.css, script.js) in the folder.

- Compress the Folder: Compress the folder into a zip file for easy uploading.

### 7. Upload the Zip File to Tiny Host

Tool: Tiny Host

Steps:

- Upload the File: Upload the zip file containing the app's files to Tiny Host.

- Get the Link: Obtain the link to the web page where the app is hosted. This link will be used to convert the web page into a smartphone app.

### 8. Convert the Web Page into a Smartphone App

Tool: Web Into App

Steps:

- Enter the Link: Enter the link obtained from Tiny Host into Web Into App.

- Customize the App: Choose a name and an icon for the app.

- Generate the APK File: Generate the APK file for the app, which can be installed on Android devices.

### 9. Install the App on the Smartphone

Steps:

- Transfer the APK File: Transfer the APK file to the smartphone, for example, using Google Drive.

- Install the App: Install the APK file on the smartphone by following the device's instructions.

## Conclusions

- Simplicity and Speed: The app creation process is quick and does not require advanced technical skills thanks to the help of ChatGPT and other tools used.

- Limitations: You cannot create complex apps like WhatsApp, but you can still create a good foundation for a simple app and enrich it later with new features.

- Monetization: Offer your app for free with in-app purchase options or subscriptions. Monetize through integrated ads in the app.

Development and programming offer numerous opportunities to create passive income, as we have analyzed in this part of the book. AI makes it possible to automate and optimize complex processes, allowing you to focus on growing and monetizing your skills.

# 4.4 Analysis and Consulting

Even analysis and consulting activities can generate passive income through the use of AI. We will use tools and platforms previously discussed to show how to best leverage these opportunities.

## Creating Dashboards and Data Analysis

Creating interactive dashboards for data analysis is a highly sought-after activity that can be enhanced by AI. Tools like Tableau and Google Data Studio allow for the creation of effective and easy-to-interpret data visualizations, facilitating decision-making for businesses.

Steps to Get Started:

1. Data Collection:

   - Collect relevant data from various sources, such as company databases, Google Analytics, social media platforms, and CRMs.

2. Creating Dashboards:

   - Use Tableau or Google Data Studio to import data and create interactive dashboards.

   - Leverage AI capabilities to analyze data and generate useful insights.

3. Customization and Automation:

   - Customize the dashboards to meet specific client needs by adding filters, charts, and other visualizations.

   - Set up automatic data updates to keep the dashboards always current.

4. Implementation and Training:

   - Share the dashboards with clients via links or by integrating them into their existing systems.

   - Provide training and support to help clients use the dashboards effectively.

5. Monetization:

   - Offer dashboard creation and maintenance services to small and medium-sized businesses.

   - Provide data-driven consulting to help clients make informed decisions.

## SEO Consulting and Optimization

Search engine optimization (SEO) is essential for improving a business's online visibility. AI can help you provide more efficient and precise SEO consulting services using tools like Ahrefs, SEMrush, and Jasper AI.

Steps to Offer SEO Consulting Services:

1. Initial Analysis:

    - Use tools like Ahrefs and SEMrush to perform a comprehensive analysis of the client's website, identifying strengths and weaknesses.

2. SEO Strategy:

    - Develop a personalized SEO strategy based on the collected data, including recommendations for site structure, keywords, and content.

3. Implementation:

    - Use Jasper AI to generate content optimized for the identified keywords.

    - Implement the recommended changes on the client's website, improving its structure and speed.

4. Monitoring and Continuous Optimization:

    - Monitor progress using SEO analysis and reporting tools.

    - Continuously optimize the SEO strategy based on results and changes in search engine algorithms.

5. Monetization:

- Offer SEO consulting packages that include initial analysis, implementation, and continuous monitoring.

- Charge monthly fees for ongoing maintenance and optimization services.

## Using AI Tools for Content Generation

Generating high-quality content is fundamental to any marketing strategy. Tools like Jasper AI can help you efficiently create articles, blog posts, product descriptions, and much more, saving time and resources.

Steps to Proceed:

1. Identifying Topics:

- Use trend analysis tools like Google Trends to identify popular and relevant topics.

2. Content Generation:

- Use Jasper AI to write articles, blog posts, product descriptions, and other content. Provide the model with a detailed brief and let the AI generate the text.

3. Content Optimization:

- Integrate relevant keywords using tools like SEMrush.

- Proofread and edit the generated content to ensure it is coherent and error-free.

4. Publication and Distribution:

- Publish the content on the client's website, blog, or e-commerce platforms.

- Promote the content through social media, email marketing, and other digital strategies.

5. Monetization:

- Offer content creation and optimization packages to small and medium-sized businesses.

- Provide content update and maintenance services to generate recurring revenue.

## Data-Driven Strategic Consulting

Data analysis is essential for making informed strategic decisions. By using AI tools, you can provide strategic consulting based on detailed data analysis, helping businesses optimize their operations and market strategies.

Steps to Provide Strategic Consulting:

1. Data Collection:

- Gather business data from various sources, such as CRMs, Google Analytics, social media platforms, and ERP systems.

2. Data Analysis:

- Use tools like Tableau and Google Data Studio to analyze the collected data.

- Leverage AI capabilities to identify trends, patterns, and anomalies in the data.

3. Strategy Development:

- Based on data analysis, develop personalized strategies to improve business operations, marketing, and sales.
- Provide practical recommendations and detailed action plans.

4. Implementation and Monitoring:

- Assist clients in implementing the recommended strategies.
- Monitor progress and adjust strategies based on the results obtained.

5. Monetization:

- Offer strategic consulting packages that include data analysis, strategy development, and continuous monitoring.
- Charge for the consulting services provided and offer maintenance and strategy update services.

## Financial Consulting and Planning

AI can also be utilized to provide financial consulting and planning services. Tools like AlphaSense and Kensho can help you analyze financial data and develop personalized investment plans for your clients.

How to Proceed:

1. Financial Data Analysis:

- Use AlphaSense to gather and analyze financial data from global sources.
- Leverage Kensho to predict market trends and identify investment opportunities.

2. Developing the Financial Plan:

- Based on the analyzed data, develop personalized investment plans for your clients.

- Recommend portfolio diversification strategies and risk management techniques.

3. Implementing the Plan:

   - Assist clients in implementing investment strategies.

   - Use trading platforms and portfolio management tools to monitor performance.

4. Monitoring and Reviewing:

   - Continuously monitor investment performance and adjust strategies based on market changes.

   - Provide periodic reports and consultations to optimize portfolio performance.

5. Monetization:

   - Offer ongoing financial consulting and planning services.

   - Charge for the consultations provided and offer maintenance and updates for financial strategies.

# 4.5 Marketing and Sales

By offering advanced tools that optimize campaigns, personalize the customer experience, and automate complex processes, artificial intelligence is transforming the landscape of marketing and sales. Here, we will explore how AI can be used to generate passive income through marketing and sales activities using the tools and platforms described in the previous chapter.

## Creation and Sale of Prompts

Creating prompts for artificial intelligence is an emerging activity that can generate passive income. Prompts are textual instructions that guide the AI in generating specific content and can be sold to individuals or businesses using content generation tools like ChatGPT.

How to proceed:

1.  Identify Market Needs:

    - Analyze market trends to identify specific content needs.

    - Use trend analysis tools like Google Trends to discover which types of content are most in demand.

2.  Create Prompts:

    - Use ChatGPT to experiment and create effective prompts. For example, create prompts to generate blog articles, product descriptions, video scripts, and more. Work thoroughly and in detail with ChatGPT to ensure the prompt is as accurate and specific as possible, perfect for your client's needs.

- Always test the prompts to ensure they produce high-quality and relevant results.

3. Sell the Prompts:

    - Set up an online store on platforms like PromptBase where you can upload and sell your prompts.

    - Promote your prompts through social media, blogs, and online communities to reach an interested audience.

4. Monetization:

    - Earn a commission on each sale of your prompts.

    - Offer prompt packages or subscriptions to generate recurring income.

This method not only allows you to earn from your knowledge and creativity but can also scale quickly as you create a diversified library of prompts.

## Selling Customized Products Online

Selling customized products is an effective way to generate passive income. Platforms like Printful, Teespring, and RedBubble allow you to create and sell a wide range of customized products, from fashion items to home accessories.

Steps to Get Started:

1. Creating Designs:

    - Use tools like Adobe Firefly to create unique and attractive designs that can be printed on various products.

- Experiment with Canva to add text, filters, and other graphic elements to your designs, making them special and distinguishable from others.

2. Uploading Designs to Products:

- Upload your designs to print-on-demand platforms like Printful, Teespring, and RedBubble.

- Select the products you want to print your designs on, such as t-shirts, mugs, posters, and more.

3. Publishing and Promoting:

- Publish your products in the online stores of the platforms.

- Use digital marketing strategies, such as creating social media posts and sending newsletters, to promote your products. Remember to use the appropriate tools for this phase of the work, as previously analyzed.

4. Managing Sales:

- Print-on-demand platforms handle production, shipping, and customer service, allowing you to focus on creating and promoting designs.

- Monitor sales and customer reviews to optimize your products and marketing strategies.

## Managing and Optimizing Advertising Campaigns

AI can significantly enhance the management and optimization of advertising campaigns, increasing the effectiveness of your marketing efforts and maximizing return on investment. Tools like Google Ads, Facebook Ads, and LinkedIn Ads offer advanced targeting and optimization features based on AI.

How to Proceed:

1. Campaign Planning:

   - Identify campaign objectives, such as increasing website traffic, generating leads, or boosting sales.

   - Define the target audience using demographic, behavioral, and interest data.

2. Creating Ads:

   - Use Jasper AI to create compelling and keyword-optimized ads.

   - Experiment with different ad formats, such as text, images, and videos.

3. Setting Up the Campaign:

   - Configure ad campaigns on platforms like Google Ads, Facebook Ads, and LinkedIn Ads.

   - Use advanced targeting features to reach the desired audience.

4. Monitoring and Optimization:

   - Monitor campaign performance using the analytics tools provided by the ad platforms.

   - Make real-time adjustments to optimize performance, such as tweaking the budget, refining targeting, and testing new creatives.

5.  Monetization:

    - Offer campaign management services to small and medium-sized businesses.

    - Charge monthly fees for ongoing campaign management and optimization services.

## Generating Social Media Content

Creating social media content can be a highly profitable activity if automated with AI. Tools like Lately.ai and Canva can help you create and schedule social media posts, analyzing performance to continuously improve engagement.

Steps to Get Started:

1.  Content Planning:

    - Use Lately.ai to analyze existing content and identify the best-performing pieces.

    - Plan an editorial calendar based on trends and performance data.

2.  Content Creation:

    - Use Canva to create original and engaging graphics, images, and videos for your social media posts.

    - Leverage Jasper AI to generate compelling text for your posts.

3.  Scheduling and Publishing:

    - Use social media management tools like Hootsuite or Buffer to schedule your posts in advance.

    - Ensure you post content regularly to maintain audience engagement.

4. Monitoring and Analysis:

- Monitor the performance of your posts using the analytics tools provided by social media platforms.

- Adjust your strategy based on engagement data and audience feedback.

5. Monetization:

- Offer social media management services to small and medium-sized businesses.

- Charge monthly fees for content creation, scheduling, and analysis services.

## Automating Affiliate Product Promotion

Affiliate marketing is an excellent way to generate passive income by promoting products from other companies. AI can automate many aspects of affiliate marketing, such as product research, content creation, and campaign optimization.

How to Proceed:

1. Product Research:

- Use affiliate research tools like EverBee to identify trending products with high commissions.

- Select relevant and high-quality products for your audience.

2. Creating Promotional Content:

- Use Jasper AI to write reviews, blog articles, promotional emails, and social media posts that promote affiliate products.

- Create engaging and high-quality graphics and images using Canva.

3. Content Distribution:

- Publish promotional content on your blog, website, and social media platforms.

- Use email marketing tools like Mailchimp to send promotional emails to your subscribers.

4. Monitoring and Optimization:

- Monitor the performance of your affiliate campaigns using analytics tools like Google Analytics.

- Continuously optimize your promotion strategies based on the collected data.

5. Monetization:

- Earn a commission on every sale generated through your affiliate links.

- Increase your income by affiliating with more products and expanding your audience.

Whether it's creating prompts, selling customized products, managing ad campaigns, generating social media content, or promoting affiliate products, AI can significantly enhance your ability to monetize your marketing activities.

# 4.6 Other Opportunities

Artificial intelligence offers a wide range of opportunities beyond the traditional activities of content creation, design, development, and marketing that we've explored so far. In this subsection, we'll delve into some additional opportunities that can generate passive or nearly passive income. Using tools and platforms described in previous chapters, we'll explore how to leverage AI for activities like automated trading, creating virtual influencers, automating business processes, and providing automated translation and transcription services.

## Automated Trading with AI and Trading Bots

Automated trading is one of the most promising applications of AI in the financial sector. By using AI-based trading bots, you can invest in financial markets such as stocks, cryptocurrencies, and forex efficiently and with minimal human intervention. Tools like AlphaSense, Kensho, and trading platforms like MetaTrader allow you to implement advanced trading strategies.

How to Proceed:

1. Select a Trading Platform:

    - Choose an automated trading platform like MetaTrader that supports the integration of AI-based trading bots.

    - Set up a trading account and verify your credentials.

2. Develop and Configure the Trading Bot:

    - Use tools like AlphaSense to collect and analyze real-time financial data.

    - Develop or purchase an AI-based trading bot, configuring it with your investment strategies.

    - Integrate the trading bot with your chosen platform, setting parameters such as risk thresholds, asset types to trade, and trading hours.

3. Monitor and Optimize:

    - Monitor the trading bot's performance using analytics tools provided by the platform.

- Make adjustments to trading strategies based on the results and market changes.

4. Monetize:

   - Earn profits generated by automated trading.

   - Consider offering your trading bot to other investors, earning a commission on its use.

Automated trading with AI not only reduces the time required to monitor the markets but can also improve the accuracy of your operations, increasing the likelihood of consistent profits.


## Creating an AI Influencer

Virtual influencers are becoming a growing trend in the digital marketing world. Developing and managing a virtual influencer using AI can open new monetization opportunities through sponsorships, collaborations, and advertising campaigns.

Earning Strategy with AI Virtual Influencers

1. Creating an AI Influencer

Tools: GitHub and Google Colab.

Steps:

1. Search "Focus GitHub" on Google and open the result.

2. Scroll down to find the "Collab" section and click "Open in Colab."

3. Generate the code and wait for the process to complete.

4. Enter the prompt to describe the desired image (e.g., "beautiful girl with red hair and brown eyes") and generate the image.

5. Select and download one of the generated images.

6.  Make further modifications using the "Face swap" and "Advanced" options to change contexts and image details.

7.  Using the AI Images

Advanced Modifications:

- Upload the image and use the "In Paint" or "Out Paint" functions to add or enhance specific details, such as accessories or clothing.

- Enter specific prompts to improve quality and add details to the image.

Examples of Scenarios:

- Create images in different contexts (e.g., at the gym, on the beach, shopping) while maintaining the consistency of the AI influencer's face.

Monetizing AI Influencers

Social Media Platforms:

- Create profiles for the AI influencer on Instagram and other social media platforms.

- Regularly post AI-generated content to increase the following.

Exclusive Content Platforms:

- Sign up the AI influencer on platforms like Fanview to offer exclusive content to fans, monetizing through monthly subscriptions (e.g., $10 per month per user).

Brand Collaborations:

- Use the AI influencer to sponsor brands and products, earning money through paid collaborations.

Market Prospects:

- AI virtual influencers are gaining popularity and can be an interesting business opportunity.

Limitations:

- Despite the potential, it is unlikely that virtual influencers will completely replace human influencers, as the latter offer authenticity and human values that virtual characters cannot replicate.

## Business Process Automation

Automating business processes can significantly improve efficiency and reduce operational costs. Using automation platforms like Zapier enhanced with AI scripts, you can automate repetitive tasks and improve the efficiency of small businesses.

Steps to Proceed:

1. Identify Processes to Automate:

    - Analyze existing business processes to identify repetitive and time-consuming tasks that can be automated.

2. Configure Automations:

    - Use Zapier to create automations (Zaps) that connect different applications and services.

    - Configure AI scripts to enhance the automations, such as data processing, automatic email sending, order management, and more.

3. Implementation and Testing:

    - Implement the automations into your business workflows.

    - Test the automations to ensure they work correctly and make any necessary adjustments.

4. Monitoring and Optimization:

    - Monitor the performance of the automations using analytics tools provided by Zapier.

    - Optimize the automations based on feedback and results.

5. Monetization:

    - Offer business process automation services to other companies, helping them improve operational efficiency.

    - Charge for configuration, implementation, and maintenance services.

Automating business processes not only frees up time for more strategic activities but also improves the accuracy and speed of business operations.

## Automated Translation and Transcription Services

AI has revolutionized translation and transcription services, offering quick and accurate solutions. Providing AI-powered automated translation and transcription services can be a source of passive income through subscription or service packages.

Steps to Proceed:

1. Service Configuration:

   - Use automatic translation tools like Google Translate or DeepL to offer fast and accurate translation services.

   - Leverage transcription tools like Otter.ai or Descript to convert audio and video into text.

2. Customization and Optimization:

   - Customize services based on specific client needs, such as translating technical documents, blog articles, meeting transcriptions, and more.

   - Use AI to improve the accuracy of translations and transcriptions, applying automatic corrections and linguistic optimizations.

3. Offer Service Packages:

- Create service packages with monthly or yearly subscription options, offering different levels of service (e.g., basic translations, specialized translations, quick transcriptions, etc.).

- Publish your offers on a professional website and promote them through digital marketing campaigns.

4. Client Management:

- Implement a customer relationship management (CRM) system to track requests, deadlines, and communications.

- Provide excellent customer service to build a loyal client base. Ensure high-quality, in-depth work by collaborating effectively with the various translation and transcription platforms at your disposal.

5. Monetization:

- Earn through recurring subscriptions and service packages.

- Expand your services to include additional languages and specific sectors to attract a broader clientele.

# Chapter 5: Ethical and Legal Aspects of AI

We've seen the potential behind the knowledge and study of using artificial intelligence (AI). With significant effort, AI can profoundly transform our world, improve quality of life, and create new business opportunities. However, with this potential comes significant responsibility. It is essential to consider the ethical and legal aspects of AI to ensure these technologies are used fairly, safely, and responsibly. In this chapter, we will explore the main ethical and legal considerations associated with AI, providing guidance on navigating these complex issues.

## 5.1 Ethical Considerations in the Use of AI

The use of AI raises numerous ethical issues that must be addressed to prevent abuses and ensure a positive impact on our society. Here are some of the main ethical considerations:

### 1. Bias and Discrimination

AI algorithms are trained on historical data. If this data contains biases, AI can perpetuate or even amplify them. For example, a hiring algorithm might discriminate against candidates based on gender or ethnicity if trained on biased historical data.

- Impact: Unfair discrimination and perpetuation of social inequalities.

- Solution: It is crucial to use representative and bias-free data to train algorithms. Companies must implement control processes to detect and correct biases in algorithms. Additionally, transparency in AI decision-making processes can help identify and mitigate potential biases.

## 2. Data Privacy and Security

AI often requires access to large amounts of personal data to function effectively. This raises concerns about data privacy and security.

- Impact: Possible privacy violations and risk of theft of sensitive data.

- Solution: Companies must implement robust security measures to protect personal data, including data encryption, controlled access, and compliance with privacy regulations like GDPR (General Data Protection Regulation) in Europe. Anonymization policies can also help protect individuals' privacy.

## 3. Transparency and Accountability

Decisions made by AI algorithms can have a significant impact on people. However, many algorithms are opaque, making it difficult to understand how decisions are made.

- Impact: Difficulty in contesting unfair decisions and lack of trust in AI technologies.

- Solution: Promoting transparency in AI models is essential. Companies should document and clearly communicate how algorithms work and what data is used. It's also important to establish who is responsible for AI decisions, ensuring there are mechanisms to challenge unjust or incorrect decisions.

## 4. Social and Economic Impacts

AI has the potential to transform entire economic sectors by automating jobs and creating new employment opportunities. However, this can also lead to unemployment and economic inequalities.

- Impact: Job loss and increased economic disparities.

- Solution: Companies and governments must work together to manage the transition to an AI-based economy. This can include retraining programs for workers affected by automation and economic policies that equitably redistribute AI benefits. Investing in education and continuous training is crucial to prepare the workforce for new opportunities created by AI.

## 5. Ethical Use of AI in Various Fields

AI is used in various sectors, each presenting specific ethical challenges. For example:

- Healthcare: Using AI for diagnosis and treatment must be done with great care to ensure patient accuracy and safety.

- Finance: Automated trading algorithms must be monitored to prevent market manipulation and unethical behavior.

- Criminal Justice: Using AI to predict criminal behavior must be managed cautiously to avoid racial profiling or other forms of discrimination.

Addressing ethical considerations in AI use is essential to ensure these technologies are used responsibly and beneficially. Companies, governments, and technology developers must collaborate to create guidelines and regulations that promote transparency, accountability, and fairness. Only then can we fully harness the potential of AI while minimizing risks and maximizing benefits for society.

## 5.2 Regulations and Laws on AI

The growing adoption of artificial intelligence (AI) has prompted governments and international organizations to develop regulations and laws to ensure these technologies are used ethically, safely, and transparently. This subchapter aims to explore the main regulations in place and the legal challenges companies face when implementing AI-based solutions.

### Importance of AI Regulation

Regulations are crucial for several reasons:

1. Protection of Personal Data: Ensuring that data collected and used by AI technologies is handled securely and respectfully, maintaining individual privacy.

2. Avoiding Discrimination and Bias: Ensuring that algorithms do not perpetuate or amplify existing biases.

3. Transparency and Accountability: Promoting transparency in AI decision-making processes and establishing who is responsible for automated decisions.

4. Safety and Reliability: Ensuring that AI technologies are safe, reliable, and do not endanger people's safety.

### Existing Regulations

1. General Data Protection Regulation (GDPR) - European Union

The GDPR is one of the most important and influential regulations on personal data protection. Although not specifically dedicated to AI, the GDPR significantly impacts how AI technologies can collect and use data.

Key Provisions:

- Consent: Companies must obtain explicit consent from individuals before collecting and using their personal data.

- Right to Access and Deletion: Individuals have the right to access their data and request its deletion.

- Transparency: Companies must clearly inform users about how their data is collected, used, and protected.

2. AI Act - European Union

The AI Act is a proposed regulation by the European Commission aimed at establishing a harmonized legal framework for AI use in Europe.

Key Provisions:

- Classification of AI Systems: AI systems are classified based on risk level (low, medium, high, unacceptable). High-risk systems, such as those used in healthcare or judicial settings, are subject to stricter regulations.

- Transparency Requirements: AI system providers must provide clear information about how algorithms work and the decisions made.

- Monitoring and Compliance: Mechanisms are in place to ensure compliance with regulations.

3. California Consumer Privacy Act (CCPA) - United States

The CCPA is a data privacy law that provides California residents with rights similar to those under the GDPR.

Key Provisions:

- Right to Know: Consumers have the right to know what personal data is collected and how it is used.

- Right to Opt-Out: Consumers can request that their personal data not be sold to third parties.

- Right to Deletion: Consumers can request the deletion of their personal data.

4. Ethical Guidelines for Trustworthy AI - European Union

These guidelines, developed by the European Commission's High-Level Expert Group on Artificial Intelligence, establish ethical principles for AI development and use.

Key Principles:

- Respect for Human Autonomy: AI should promote, not diminish, human autonomy.

- Prevention of Harm: AI should be designed to prevent harm and ensure safety.

- Fairness: AI should promote fairness and avoid discrimination.

- Explainability: AI decisions should be understandable and explainable to users.

## Legal Challenges and Compliance

Companies developing or using AI technologies face several legal challenges to ensure compliance with existing regulations:

1. Data Management

- Data Collection and Storage: Companies must ensure that data is collected and stored in compliance with privacy regulations. This includes obtaining user consent and protecting sensitive data.

- Data Sharing: Clear policies must be established for sharing data with third parties, ensuring that such practices are transparent and comply with existing laws.

2. Algorithm Transparency

- Documentation and Explainability: Companies must document how their AI algorithms work and ensure that automated decisions can be clearly explained to users.

- Auditing and Monitoring: It is essential to implement regular auditing processes to monitor the functioning of algorithms and ensure they are bias-free and compliant with regulations.

3. Responsibility and Governance

- Decision Accountability: Companies must establish who is responsible for decisions made by AI algorithms, ensuring there are mechanisms to contest unfair or erroneous decisions.

- AI Governance: Internal governance structures are needed to oversee the use of AI and ensure compliance with ethical and legal standards.

## International Initiatives and Future Regulations

Beyond existing regulations, several international initiatives are underway to develop guidelines and future regulations for AI:

1. OECD Principles on AI The Organisation for Economic Co-operation and Development (OECD) has developed principles for AI that promote the responsible and sustainable use of AI technologies.

Key Principles:

- Inclusivity and Sustainability: AI should contribute to sustainable development and inclusivity.

- Transparency and Explainability: Decisions made by AI should be transparent and explainable.

- Accountability: Stakeholders involved in the development and use of AI should be accountable for their actions.

2. United Nations Initiatives The United Nations is working on global guidelines for AI, aiming to promote the ethical and safe use of AI technologies worldwide.

Objectives:

- Promote Fairness and Justice: Ensure that AI does not perpetuate social inequalities or discrimination.

- Human Rights Protection: Ensure that AI is used in a manner that respects fundamental human rights.

- Sustainability: Encourage the use of AI to address global challenges such as climate change and poverty.

Regulations and laws on AI are crucial to ensure that these technologies are used safely, ethically, and responsibly. Companies must stay updated on existing and future regulations, implementing solid compliance and governance practices to avoid legal risks and ensure consumer trust.

# 5.3 Data Privacy and Security

In the digital era, data privacy and security have become fundamental concerns, especially with the increasing use of artificial intelligence (AI). AI technologies often require access to large amounts of personal data to function effectively, raising important questions about how this data is collected, stored, used, and protected. In this subsection, we will explore best practices for ensuring data privacy and security when using AI.

### Importance of Data Privacy and Security

Protecting personal data is essential for several reasons:

1. Respecting Individual Rights: Individuals have the right to know how their data is used and to expect that this data is handled respectfully and securely.

2. Regulatory Compliance: Companies must adhere to privacy laws, such as GDPR in Europe and CCPA in California, to avoid legal penalties.

3. Consumer Trust: Protecting data is crucial for maintaining consumer trust, as people are increasingly concerned about the privacy of their personal information.

4. Preventing Fraud and Data Breaches: Good data security management can prevent fraud, data breaches, and other cybersecurity risks.

## Data Collection and Storage

Managing data collection and storage with care is critical to ensure privacy and security.

1. Data Collection

- Informed Consent: Companies must obtain explicit consent from individuals before collecting their personal data. This includes clearly informing users about what data is collected, how it will be used, and how long it will be retained.

- Data Minimization: Collect only the data necessary for the specific purpose. Avoid collecting superfluous data to reduce the risk of breaches and simplify privacy management.

- Transparency: Inform users about how their data will be used, with whom it will be shared, and what security measures will be taken to protect it.

2. Data Storage

- Encryption: Personal data should be encrypted both in transit (during transfer) and at rest (when stored). Encryption makes the data unreadable to anyone without the decryption key.

- Limited Access: Implement strict access controls to ensure that only authorized personnel can access sensitive data. Use two-factor authentication and role-based controls to limit data access.

- Secure Backups: Regularly perform secure backups of data to prevent data loss in the event of cyberattacks or hardware failures.

## Data Usage

Once data is collected and securely stored, it must be used in compliance with privacy regulations and security best practices.

1. Anonymization and Pseudonymization

- Anonymization: Transform personal data so that it cannot be linked back to a specific individual. This may include removing or altering identifying information.

- Pseudonymization: Replace identifying information with pseudonyms. Unlike anonymization, pseudonymization allows re-identification of individuals through the use of decryption keys but reduces the risk of accidental identification.

2.Purpose Limitation

- Limited Use: Use personal data only for the specific purposes for which it was collected. Avoid using data for undeclared purposes without user consent.

- Retention Period: Retain personal data only for as long as necessary to achieve the purposes for which it was collected. After this period, data should be deleted or anonymized.

3. Monitoring and Auditing

- Continuous Monitoring: Implement monitoring systems to detect and respond quickly to any data security breaches. Use intrusion detection tools and behavior analysis to identify suspicious activities.

- Regular Audits: Conduct regular audits to verify compliance with privacy regulations and company data security policies. Audits can help identify and correct vulnerabilities before they can be exploited.

## Data Protection Against Threats

Protecting data requires a proactive approach to prevent and mitigate threats.

1. Employee Training

- Security Awareness: Train staff on best data security practices and raise awareness about cybersecurity threats. Ensure that all employees understand the importance of data protection and know how to recognize and respond to threats.

- Incident Response Procedures: Establish clear procedures for responding to data security incidents, including steps to take in the event of a data breach.

2. Advanced Security Technologies

- Firewalls and Intrusion Prevention Systems: Use firewalls and intrusion prevention systems to protect corporate networks from unauthorized access and cyber attacks.

- Antivirus and Antimalware Software: Install and maintain up-to-date antivirus and antimalware software to protect corporate systems from cyber threats.

3. Access and Control Policies

- Access Policies: Implement access policies based on the principle of least privilege, ensuring that employees only have access to the data and systems necessary to perform their duties.

- Physical Access Controls: Protect sensitive data from unauthorized physical access using physical security measures such as locks, access badges, and surveillance cameras.

- 

## Compliance with Privacy Regulations

Companies must ensure compliance with local and international privacy regulations to avoid legal penalties and maintain consumer trust.

1. General Data Protection Regulation (GDPR) - European Union

Key Provisions:

- Informed Consent: Obtain explicit consent from users before collecting and using their data.

- Right of Access and Erasure: Users have the right to access their data and request its deletion.

- Data Protection Officer (DPO): Appoint a DPO to ensure compliance with privacy regulations and manage user requests.

2. California Consumer Privacy Act (CCPA) - United States

Key Provisions:

- Right to Know: Inform consumers about the data collected and how it is used.

- Right to Opt-Out: Allow consumers to opt out of having their data sold to third parties.

- Right to Deletion: Allow consumers to request the deletion of their personal data.

Data privacy and security are essential components for the responsible use of artificial intelligence. Implementing robust data management practices, threat protection measures, and regulatory compliance not only protects individuals but also strengthens consumer trust and corporate reputation. As AI continues to evolve, companies must remain vigilant and proactive in managing data privacy and security, ensuring a secure and privacy-respecting digital future.

# Chapter 6: Additional Resources and Continuing Education

As we come to the end of this book, it's clear that our journey in learning about AI and its countless applications is far from over. Artificial Intelligence (AI) is a rapidly evolving field that demands constant updates to one's skills and knowledge. To stay competitive and fully leverage the opportunities offered by AI, it's crucial to invest in continuous education and stay informed about the latest innovations. In this chapter, we will explore additional resources such as books, online courses, and learning communities, as well as the best strategies to stay updated on the latest trends and developments in the field of AI.

## 6.1 Books and Courses

One of the best ways to deepen your knowledge of AI is through reading books and participating in online courses. Here is a list of resources that can help you improve your skills and stay up to date.

### Recommended Books

1. "Artificial Intelligence: A Modern Approach" by Stuart Russell and Peter Norvig

   - This book is considered the bible of AI and offers a comprehensive overview of the principles and techniques of artificial intelligence.

2. "Deep Learning" by Ian Goodfellow, Yoshua Bengio, and Aaron Courville

- A fundamental book for those who want to delve into deep learning, written by some of the foremost experts in the field.

3. "Superintelligence: Paths, Dangers, Strategies" by Nick Bostrom

   - Explores the future implications of AI and the potential risks associated with the development of superintelligence.

4. "Life 3.0: Being Human in the Age of Artificial Intelligence" by Max Tegmark

   - An accessible introduction to AI and its potential consequences on society.

5. "Hands-On Machine Learning with Scikit-Learn, Keras, and TensorFlow" by Aurélien Géron

   - An excellent practical resource for those who want to learn how to implement machine learning and deep learning algorithms.

## Online Courses

1. Coursera - Machine Learning by Andrew Ng

   - An introductory course offered by Coursera and taught by Andrew Ng, one of the pioneers of machine learning.

2. edX - Professional Certificate in Artificial Intelligence by IBM

   - A professional certification program that covers various aspects of AI, from machine learning to computer vision.

3. Udacity - Artificial Intelligence Nanodegree

   - An intensive training program that prepares students to become AI experts through practical projects and interactive lessons.

4. Fast.ai - Practical Deep Learning for Coders

   - A free course focused on teaching deep learning in a practical and accessible way.

5. Kaggle - Learn

   - Kaggle offers a series of free mini-courses covering various aspects of machine learning and data science, ideal for those who want to learn by doing.

## Learning Communities

Engaging with online learning communities can be highly beneficial for staying motivated and updated. Some of the main communities include:

- Kaggle: A platform for machine learning competitions and a community of data scientists.

- Stack Overflow: A Q&A site for programmers, where you can find solutions to specific AI-related problems.

- Reddit - r/MachineLearning: An active subreddit discussing the latest research and trends in AI.

- AI Conferences: Attending AI conferences such as NeurIPS, ICML, and CVPR offers the opportunity to learn from the brightest minds in the field.

## 6.2 Staying Updated on Innovations

The field of AI is constantly evolving, with new discoveries and innovations emerging regularly. Here are some strategies to stay updated on the latest developments in artificial intelligence.

1.  Follow Blogs and Newsletters

    *   Towards Data Science: A blog that publishes articles and tutorials on various aspects of AI and machine learning.

    *   The Batch by deeplearning.ai: A weekly newsletter summarizing the latest news and research in AI.

    *   AI Weekly: A newsletter providing weekly updates on AI research, tools, and applications.

2.  Attend Webinars and Online Conferences

Many AI events are now available online, making it easier to participate from anywhere in the world. Attending webinars and conferences allows you to hear from industry experts and discover the latest trends and innovations.

3. Use Social Media Platforms

- LinkedIn: Follow industry leaders and AI-specialized companies to stay updated on the latest news and job opportunities.

- X (formerly Twitter): Follow hashtags like #AI, #MachineLearning, and #DeepLearning to find new articles, research, and discussions.

4. Subscribe to Journals and Academic Publications

- Journal of Artificial Intelligence Research (JAIR): A leading academic publication covering all aspects of AI.

- Machine Learning Journal: Another important publication offering research articles on machine learning techniques and applications.

5. Join Study Groups and Workshops

Study groups and workshops provide opportunities to delve into specific topics and work on practical projects with other industry professionals.

6. Collaborate on Open Source Projects

Participating in open source projects on platforms like GitHub can be an excellent way to gain practical experience and contribute to the AI community.

Staying updated in the field of artificial intelligence requires a continuous commitment to learning and education. By utilizing available resources such as books, online courses, learning communities, and update tools, you can keep pace with the latest innovations and developments. Investing in your education and staying informed about emerging trends will not only enhance your skills but also open new business and career opportunities in the dynamic world of AI.

# Chapter 7: Conclusions and the Future of AI

In this concluding chapter, we will explore predictions for the future of AI, how to prepare for upcoming changes, and which strategies to adopt to ensure success in a technology-dominated world. Finally, we will discuss an important career opportunity: developing advanced skills in AI dialogue.

## 7.1 Predictions for the Future of Artificial Intelligence

The future of AI promises to be incredibly dynamic and influential across various sectors. Experts predict that AI will continue to evolve, becoming increasingly integrated into our daily lives. Here are some of the key trends and predictions:

1. Advanced Automation: AI will continue to enhance the automation of repetitive and complex tasks, leading to increased productivity and operational efficiency in many industries. This will include the automation of business processes, human resources management, and industrial production.

2. Generative Artificial Intelligence: Generative AI tools, used to create texts, images, and music, will become even more sophisticated. These tools will not only boost human creativity but also revolutionize industries such as entertainment, marketing, and education.

3. Improvements in Health and Medicine: AI will play a crucial role in improving healthcare, from early disease

diagnosis to personalized treatments and patient management. Machine learning algorithms will analyze large amounts of medical data to identify patterns and provide clinical recommendations.

4. Expansion of Augmented and Virtual Reality: With the help of AI, augmented reality (AR) and virtual reality (VR) will become more immersive and interactive. These technologies will have significant applications in education, entertainment, professional training, and real estate.

5. Ethics and Regulation: As AI becomes more pervasive, there will be growing attention to ethical issues and the need for appropriate regulations. Discussions on transparency, accountability, and fairness will become increasingly central, influencing the development and adoption of AI.

## 7.2 Preparing for Future Changes

Preparing for the future of AI requires a continuous commitment to learning and adaptation. We have already explored many opportunities to stay informed and updated in the previous chapter. Here are additional strategies to keep pace with changes:

1. Continuous Education: As emphasized before, investing in continuous learning and staying updated on the latest AI trends is crucial. Participating in online courses, webinars, and conferences can help keep your skills current.

2. Adaptability and Flexibility: Being ready to adapt quickly to technological changes is essential. Companies and

individuals must be willing to experiment with new technologies and adjust their operational strategies based on market needs.

3. Interdisciplinary Collaboration: AI is a field that benefits from collaboration across various disciplines. Engineers, scientists, ethicists, and business professionals must work together to develop innovative and responsible solutions.

4. Ethical Awareness: Understanding the ethical implications of AI is fundamental to ensure these technologies are used fairly and responsibly. This includes managing biases in algorithms and protecting data privacy.

# 7.3 Strategies for Success

To succeed in an AI-dominated world, it is important to develop effective strategies that maximize the opportunities offered by technology. One of the most valuable skills in this context is the ability to interact knowledgeably with AI.

## Developing Skills in AI Dialogue

An important earning opportunity lies in learning to interact effectively with AI models. This includes the ability to write precise prompts and an in-depth understanding of AI tools to fully exploit their potential.

1. Learning to Write Effective Prompts:

   - Understanding AI Models: Knowing how AI models work is crucial for writing effective prompts. A well-formulated prompt can yield more precise and useful responses.

   - Practice and Experimentation: Experiment with different types of prompts to see which ones produce the best results. Document your successes and failures to continuously improve.

   - Utilizing AI Tools: The more familiar you are with the functionalities of these tools, the better you can leverage them.

2. Conscious Interaction with AI:

   - In-Depth Study of Tools: Spend time studying and thoroughly understanding the AI tools you use. This includes reading documentation, participating in user communities, and hands-on experimentation.

   - Adaptability to New Technologies: Stay updated on the latest innovations and developments in AI. Being at the forefront will allow you to capitalize on new opportunities ahead of the competition.

While much of this book has focused on the professional role of content creators leveraging AI, it is important to consider, in this concluding part, the opportunities offered by a new role: that of a business consultant specializing in artificial intelligence.

## The AI Business Consultant

As the final point of this book, we want to introduce a new and necessary professional role: the AI business consultant. An AI business consultant helps companies integrate artificial intelligence solutions into their operational processes, enhancing efficiency, productivity, and competitiveness. This professional role requires a combination of technical, strategic, and communication skills. Here are some key aspects of the role:

1. Business Needs Analysis:

    - The consultant starts with an in-depth analysis of the business needs, identifying areas where AI can add value. This can include process automation, data analysis, customer service improvement, and more.

    - Understanding the specific market dynamics of the client company is crucial to proposing tailored solutions.

2. Development of Customized Solutions:

    - Based on the analysis, the consultant develops tailored solutions that integrate appropriate AI tools and technologies. This may involve selecting software, designing custom algorithms, and integrating with existing systems.

    - Using tools like Google Colab and GitHub to prototype and test solutions quickly.

3. Implementation and Training:

- Once the solutions are developed, the consultant guides the implementation, ensuring a smooth integration and that staff are adequately trained to use the new technologies.

- Organizing workshops and training sessions to ensure the business team understands how to use AI tools effectively.

4. Monitoring and Optimization:

- After implementation, the consultant monitors the performance of AI solutions, making adjustments and optimizations based on the results and user feedback.

- Providing detailed reports that show the impact of AI solutions on business processes and suggesting further improvements.

5. Ongoing Strategic Consulting:

- The consultant continues to provide strategic support, helping the company stay competitive and leverage new AI opportunities as they arise.

- Staying updated on the latest AI innovations to offer informed and cutting-edge advice.

## Earning Opportunities for AI Business Consultants

Being an AI business consultant offers numerous earning opportunities. Here's how this role can monetize their expertise:

1. Hourly or Project-Based Rates:

- Consultants can charge for their services on an hourly basis or per project. Complex and long-term projects can lead to significant earnings.

2. Maintenance and Support Contracts:

   - Offering maintenance and continuous support contracts to client companies to ensure AI solutions remain effective and up-to-date.

3. Workshops and Training:

   - Organizing workshops and training sessions for companies, monetizing through ticket sales or training packages.

4. Partnerships and Collaborations:

   - Collaborating with technology providers and AI platforms to offer integrated solutions, earning commissions on sales or subscriptions.

We have reached the end of this book, a book that we hope has helped you understand and explore the opportunities AI offers to generate income in numerous fields. The future of artificial intelligence is full of promise and opportunity. Preparing for future changes, developing advanced skills in AI dialogue, and adopting conscious adaptation strategies are essential steps to succeed in this new technological landscape. With AI the possibilities for innovation and growth are endless, and the potential to generate income is within reach for anyone willing to invest in their development and understanding of these powerful technologies.

Made in the USA
Columbia, SC
14 June 2025

59407123R00089